Brain Patterns

CLEVER COLORING

BRAIN PATTERNS
CLEVER COLORING
by Digi Green Publishing

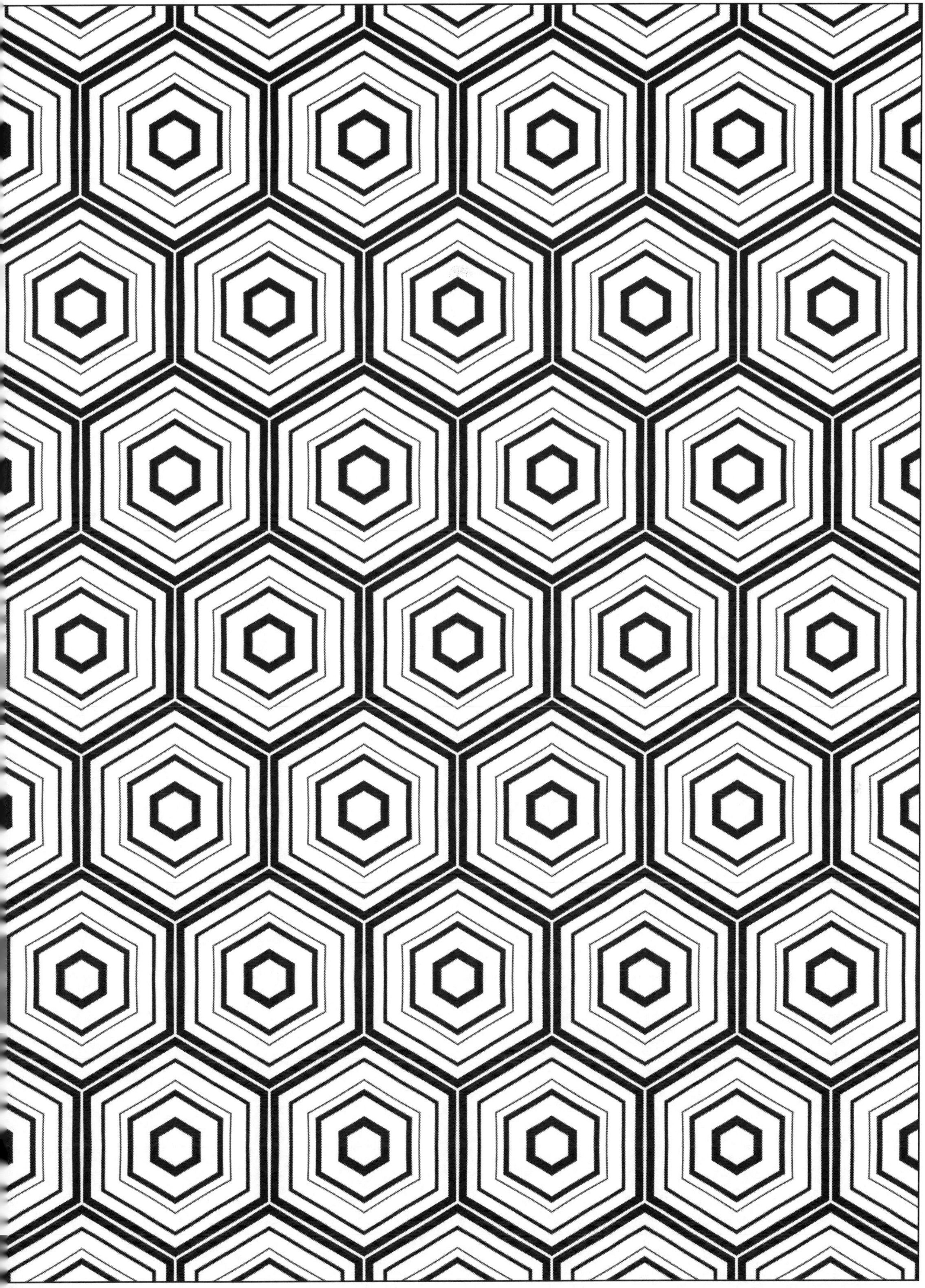

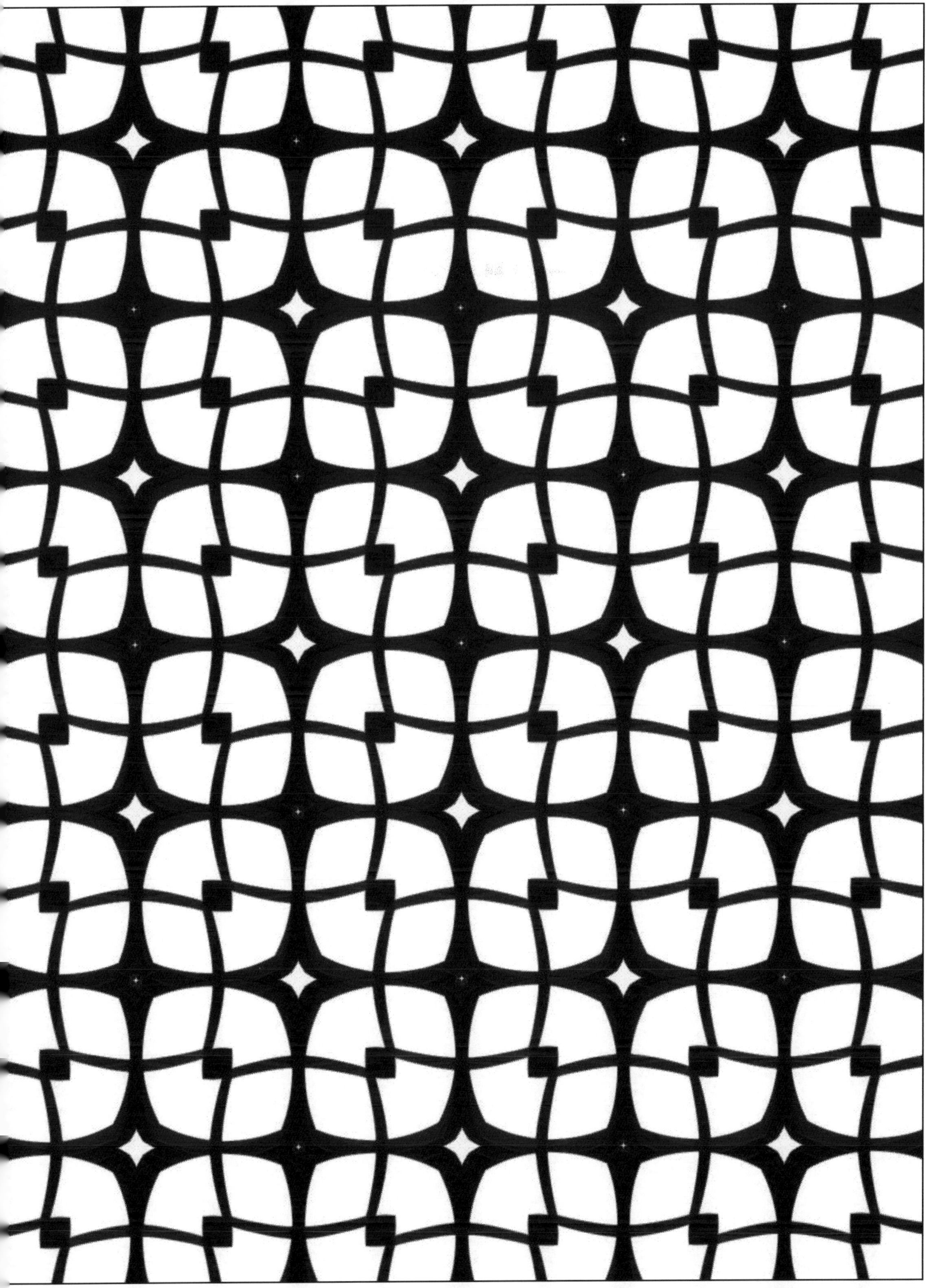

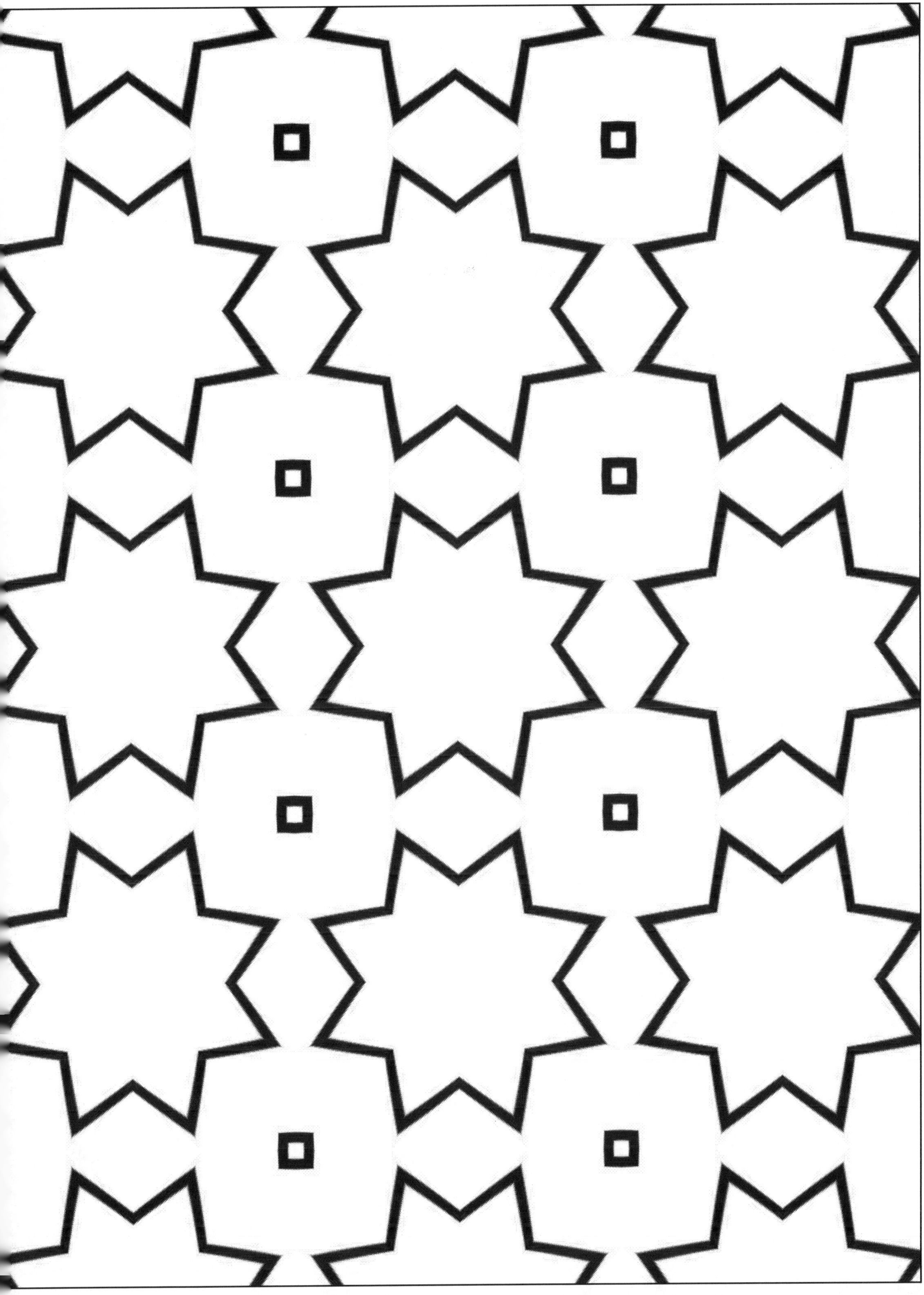

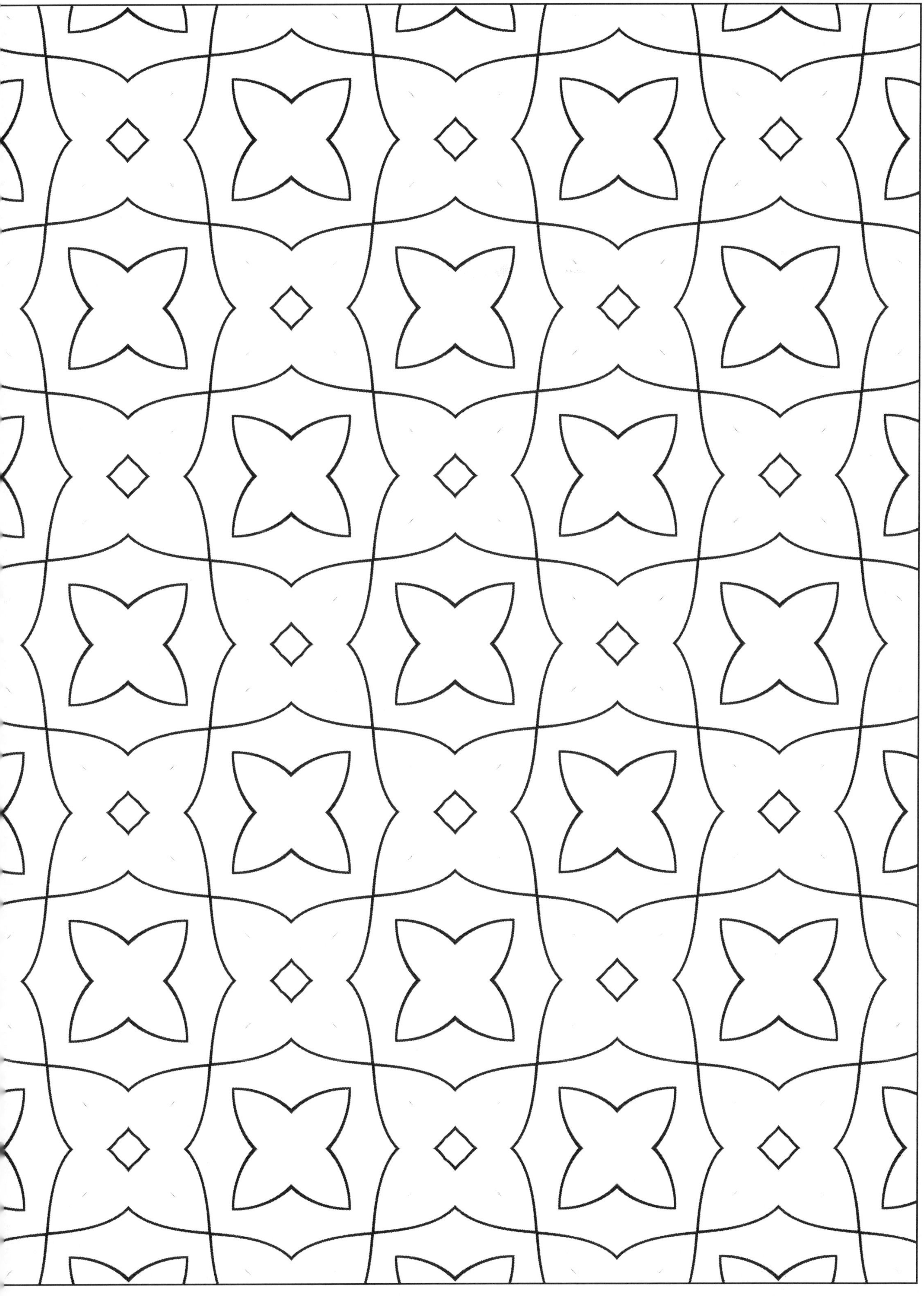

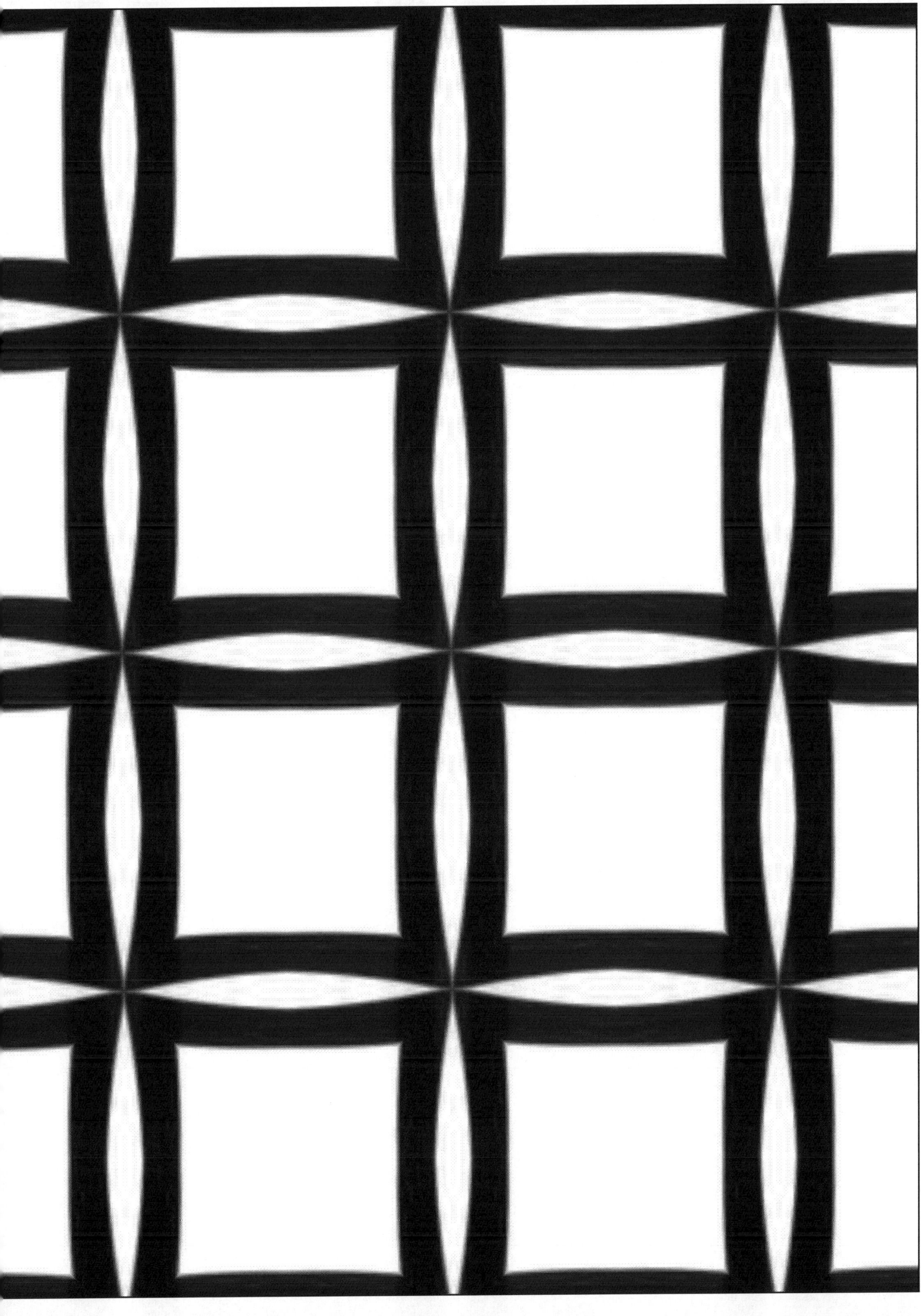

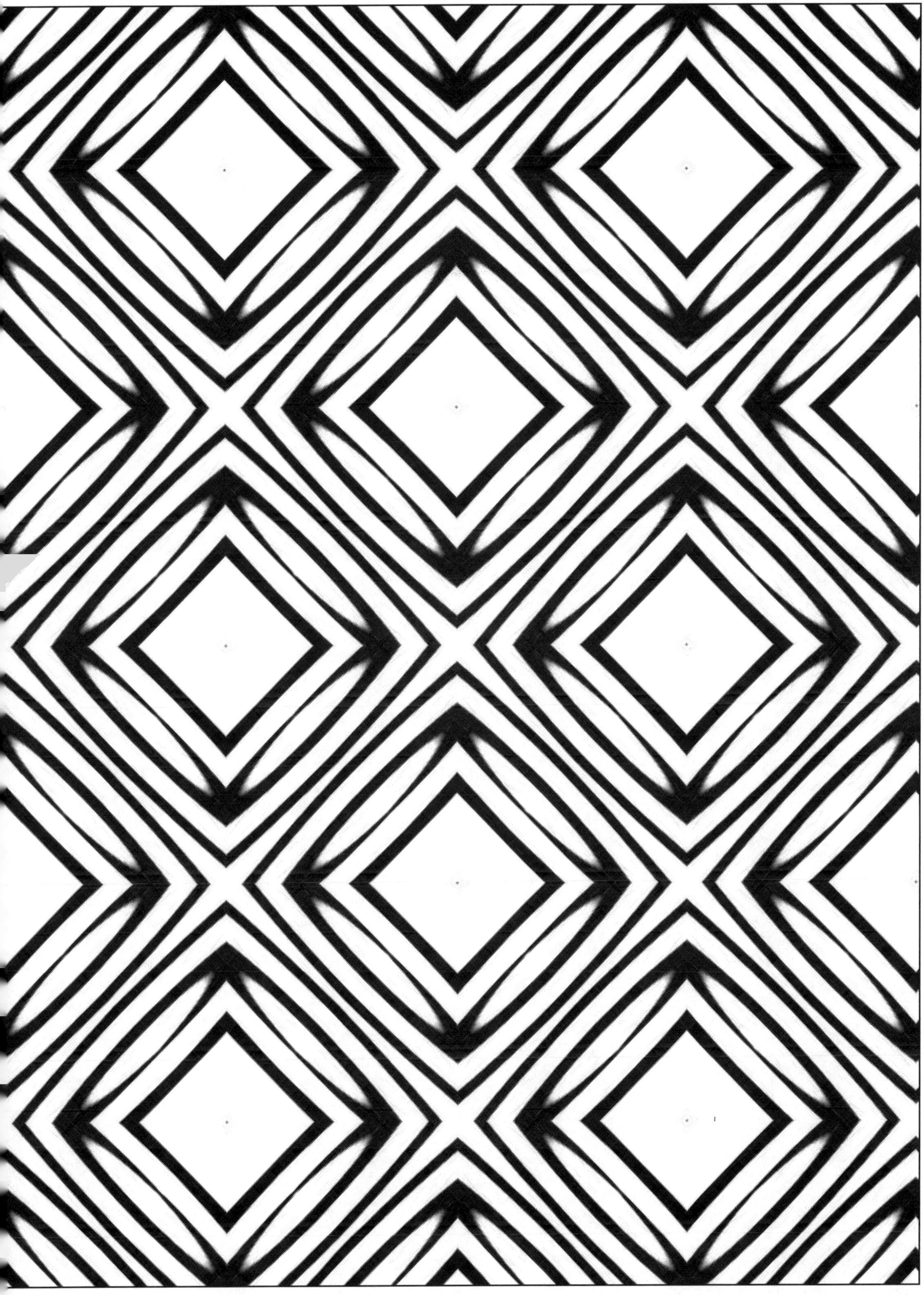

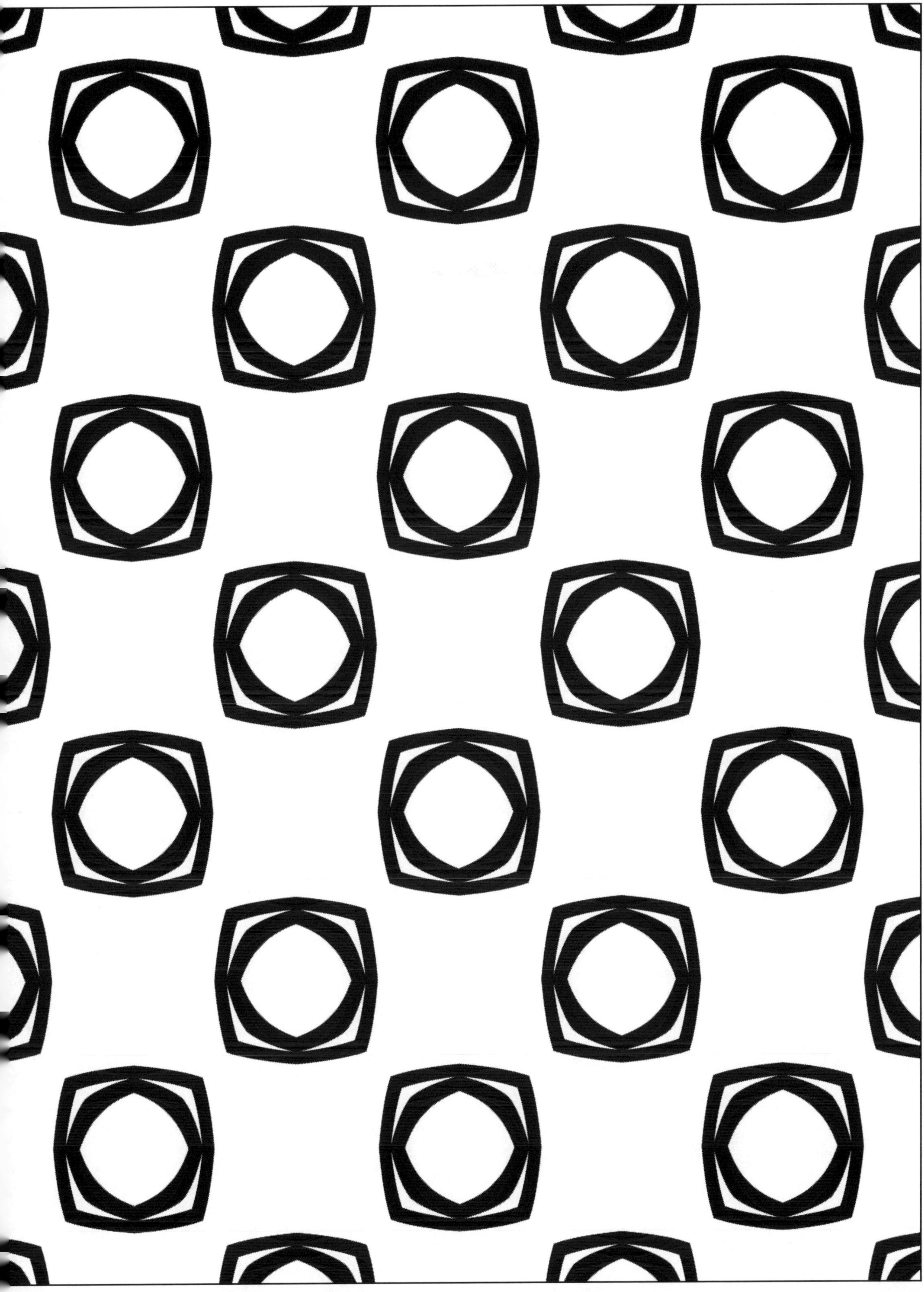

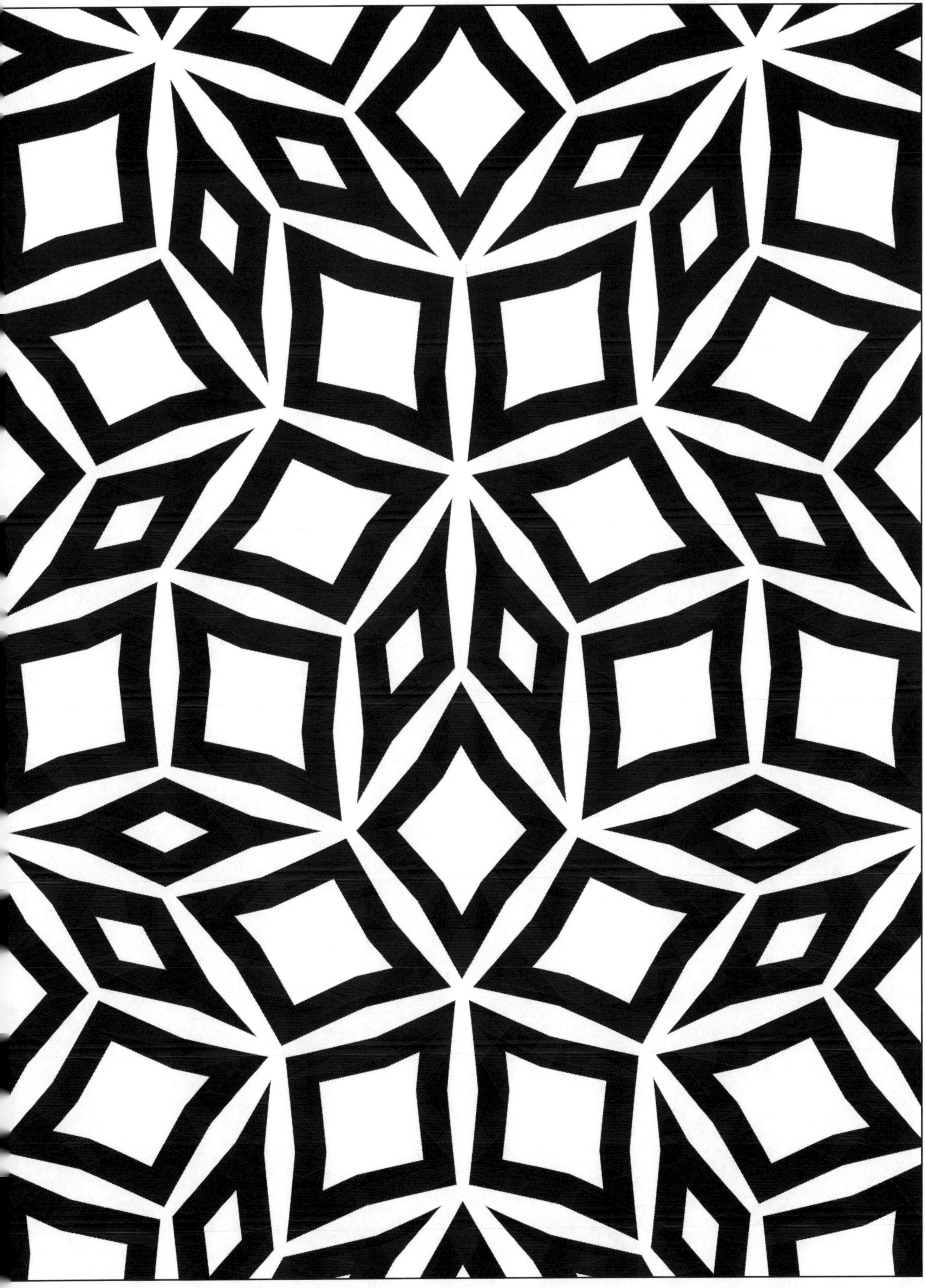

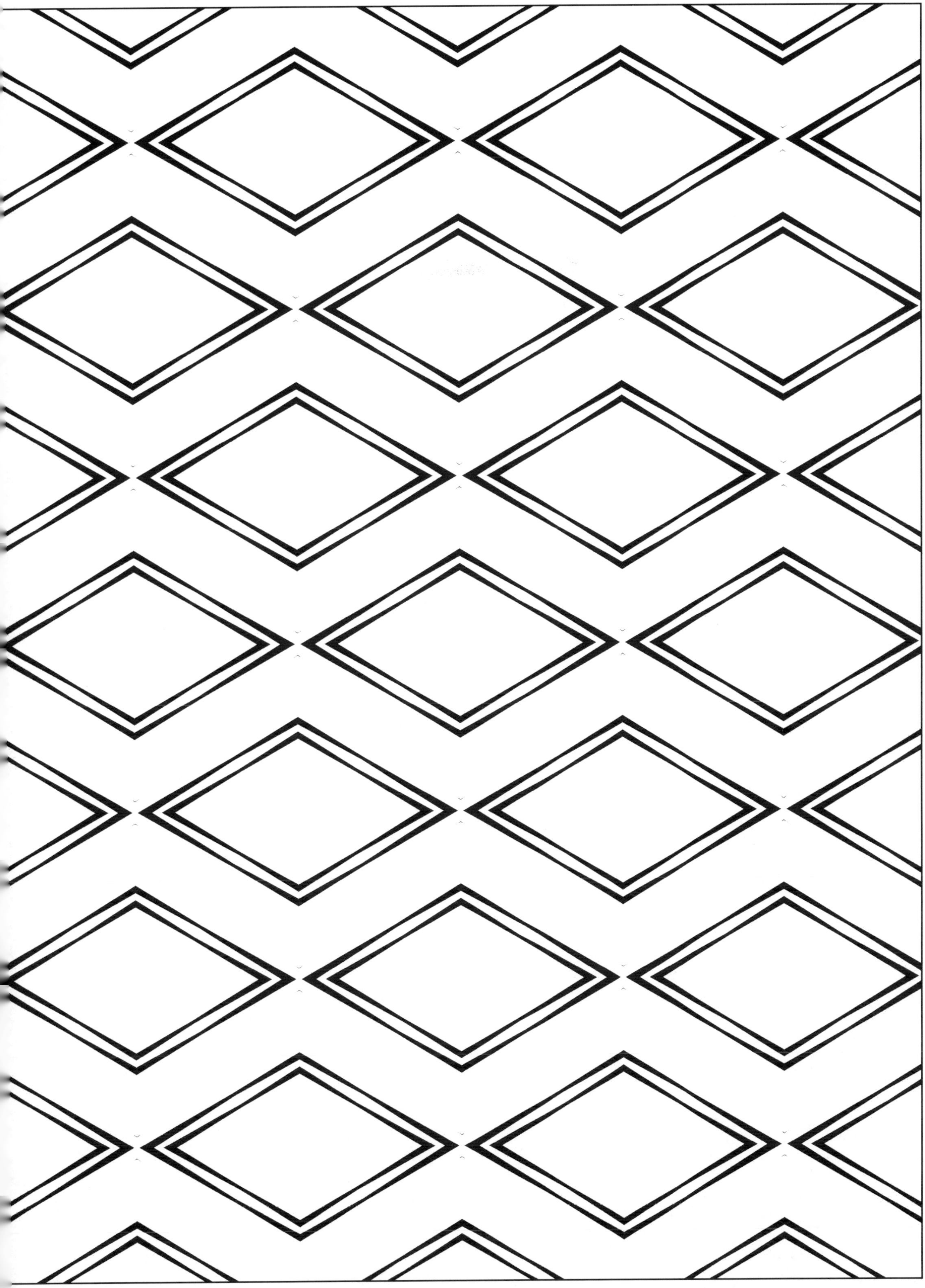

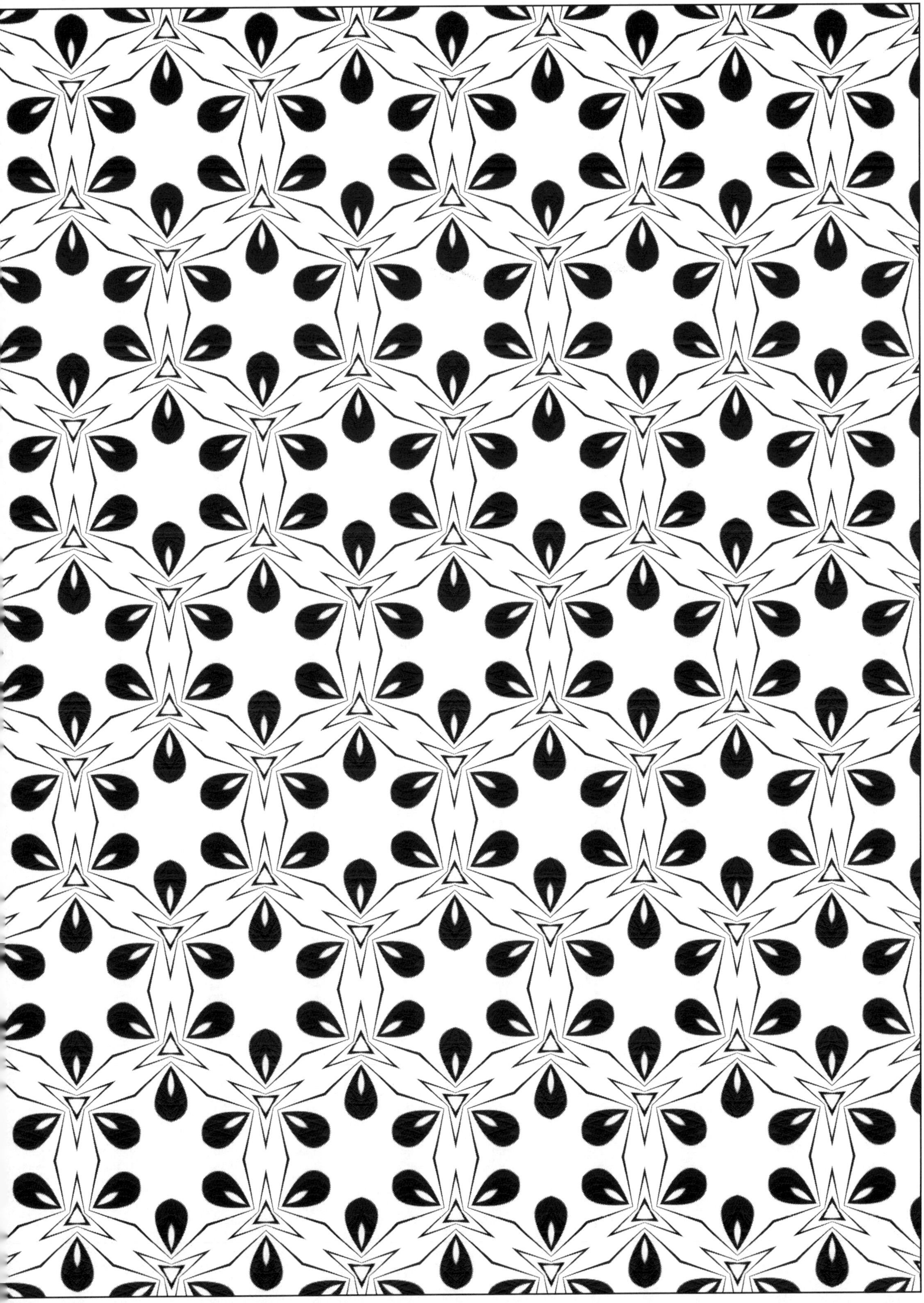

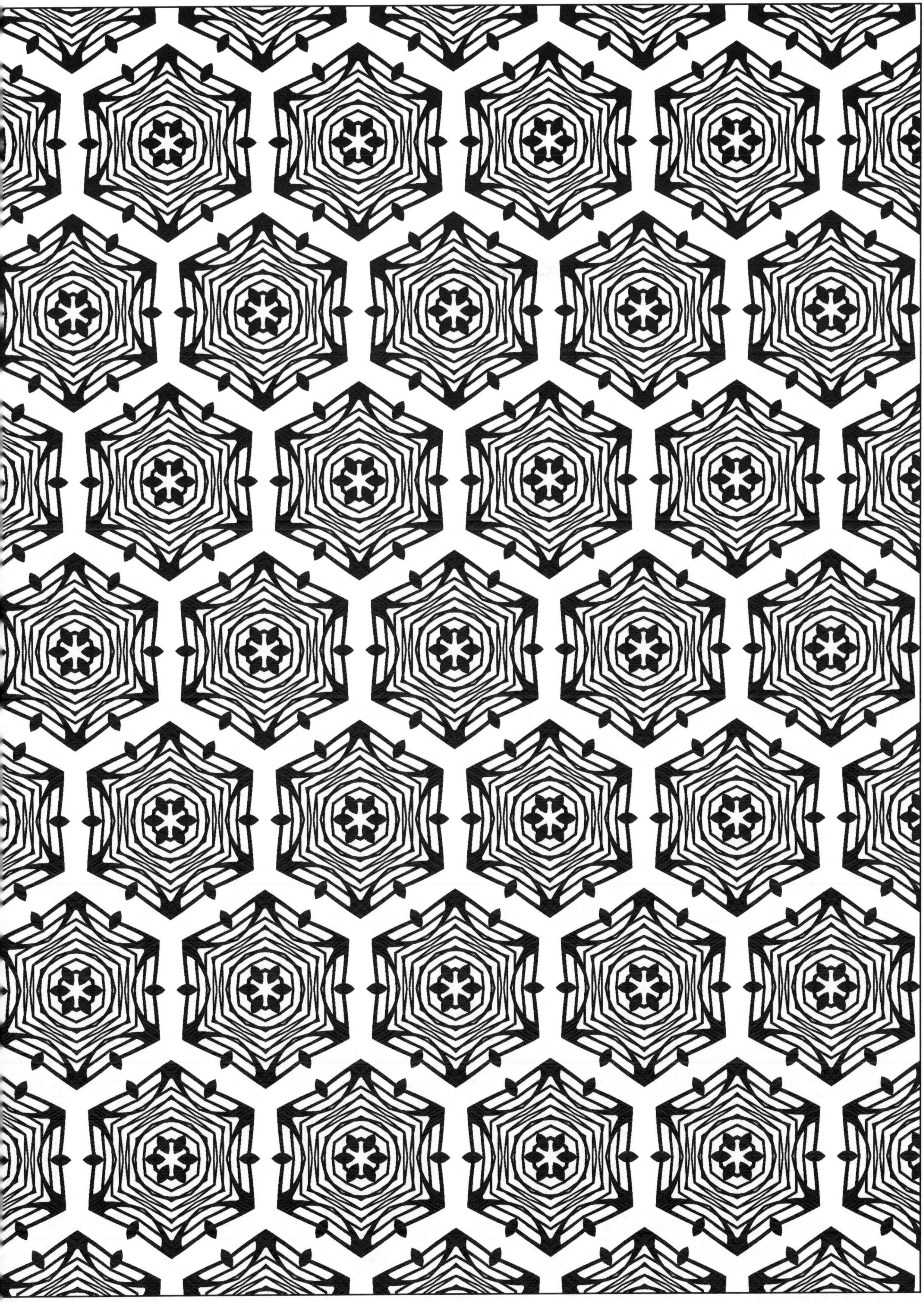

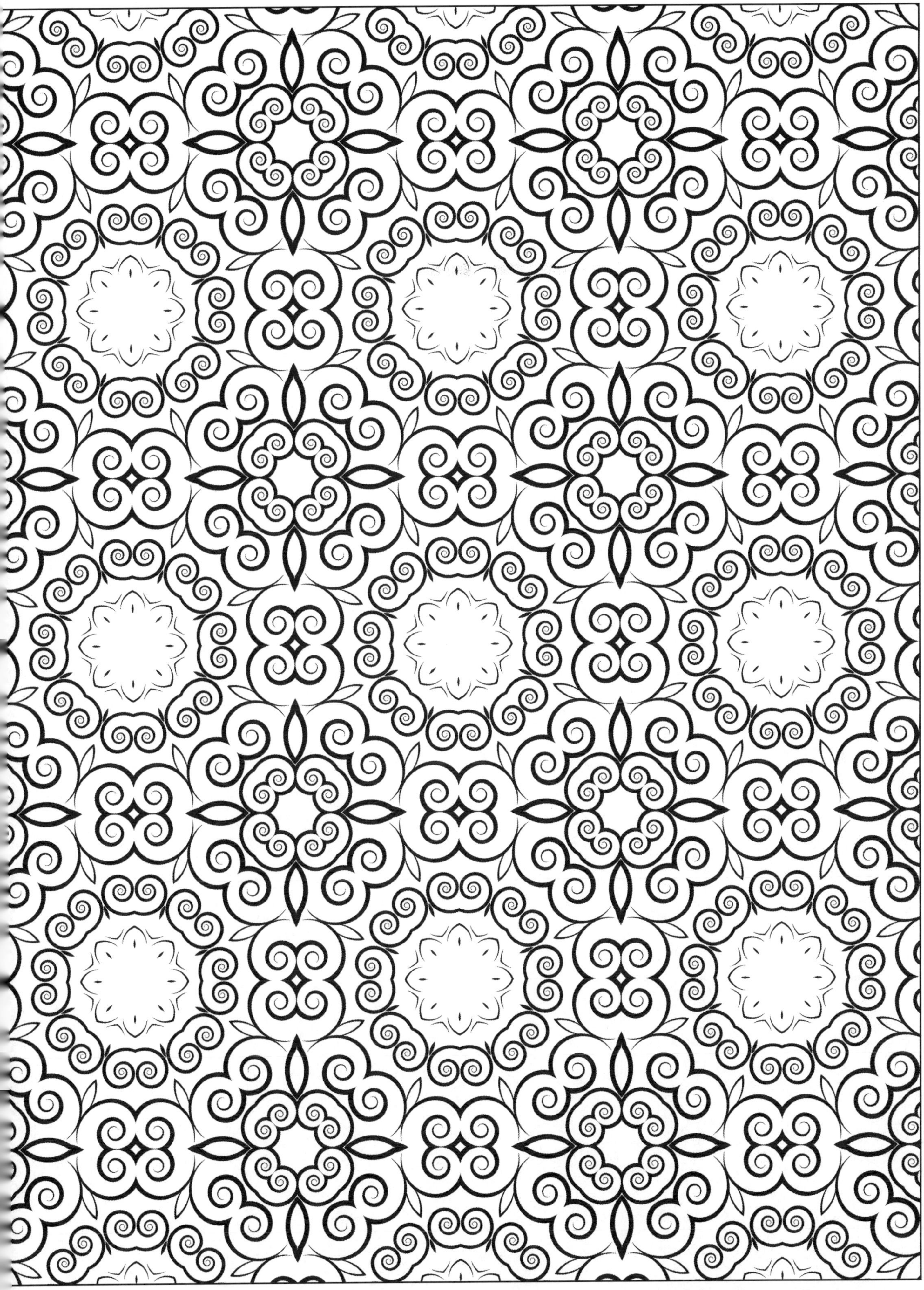

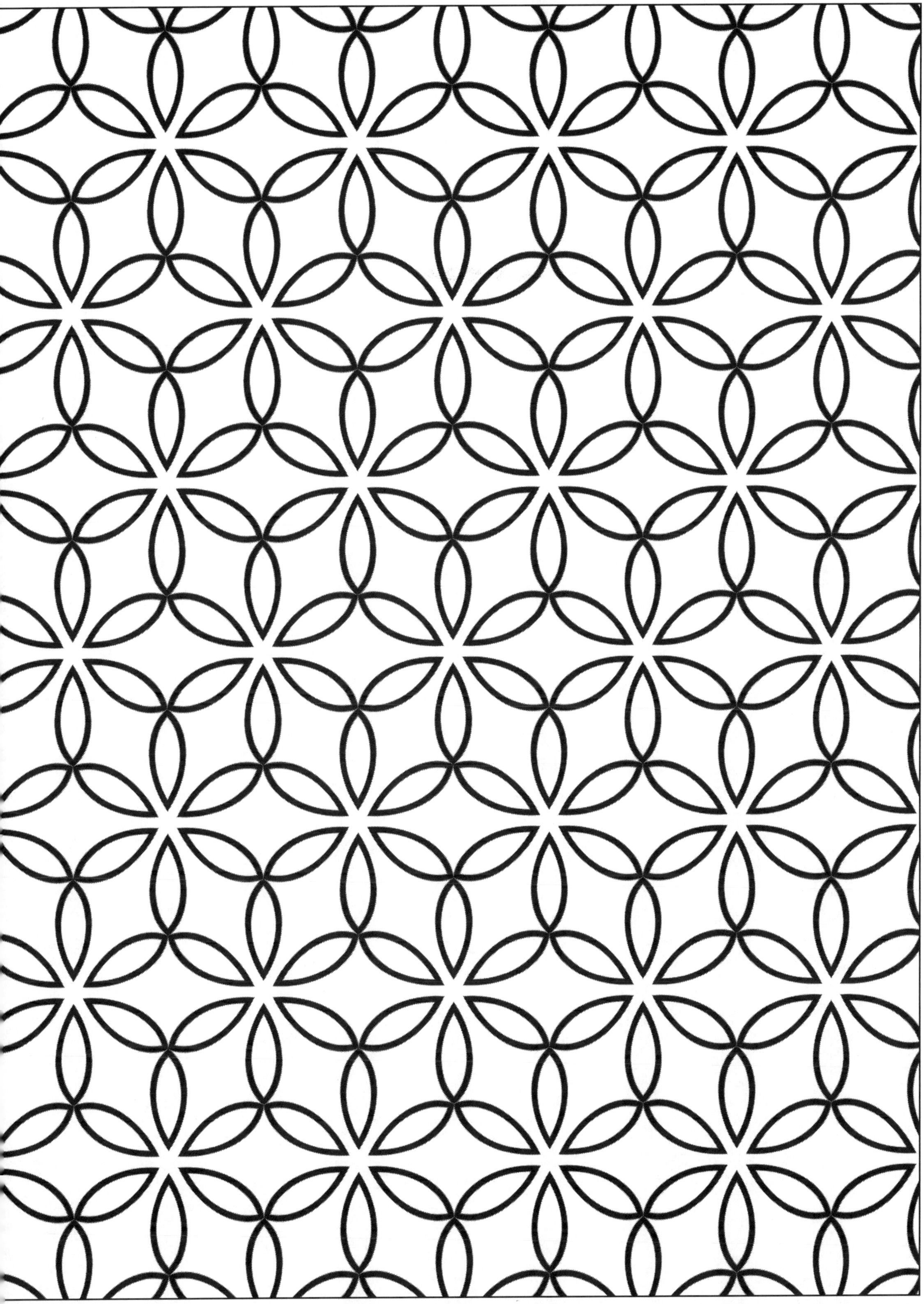

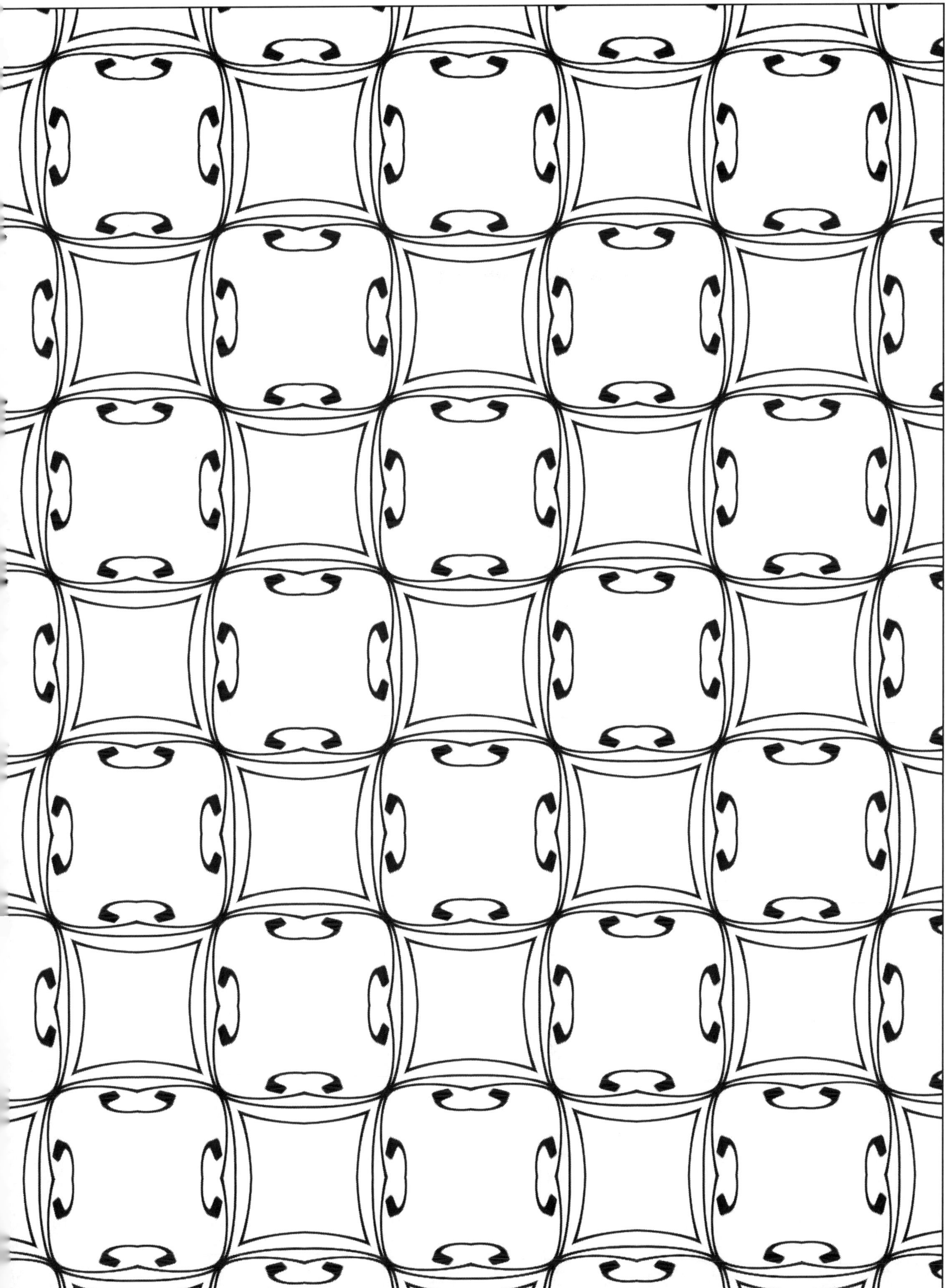

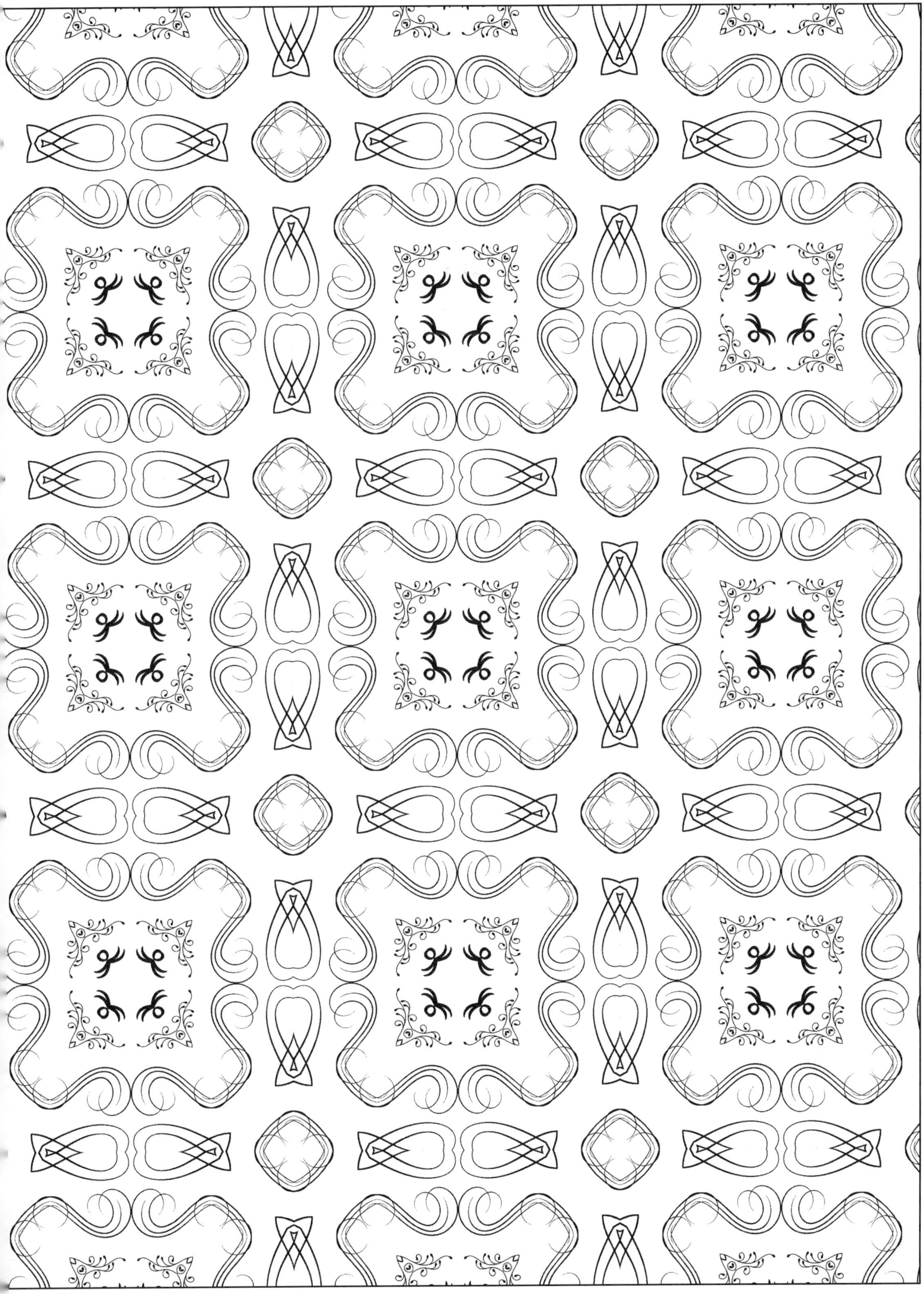

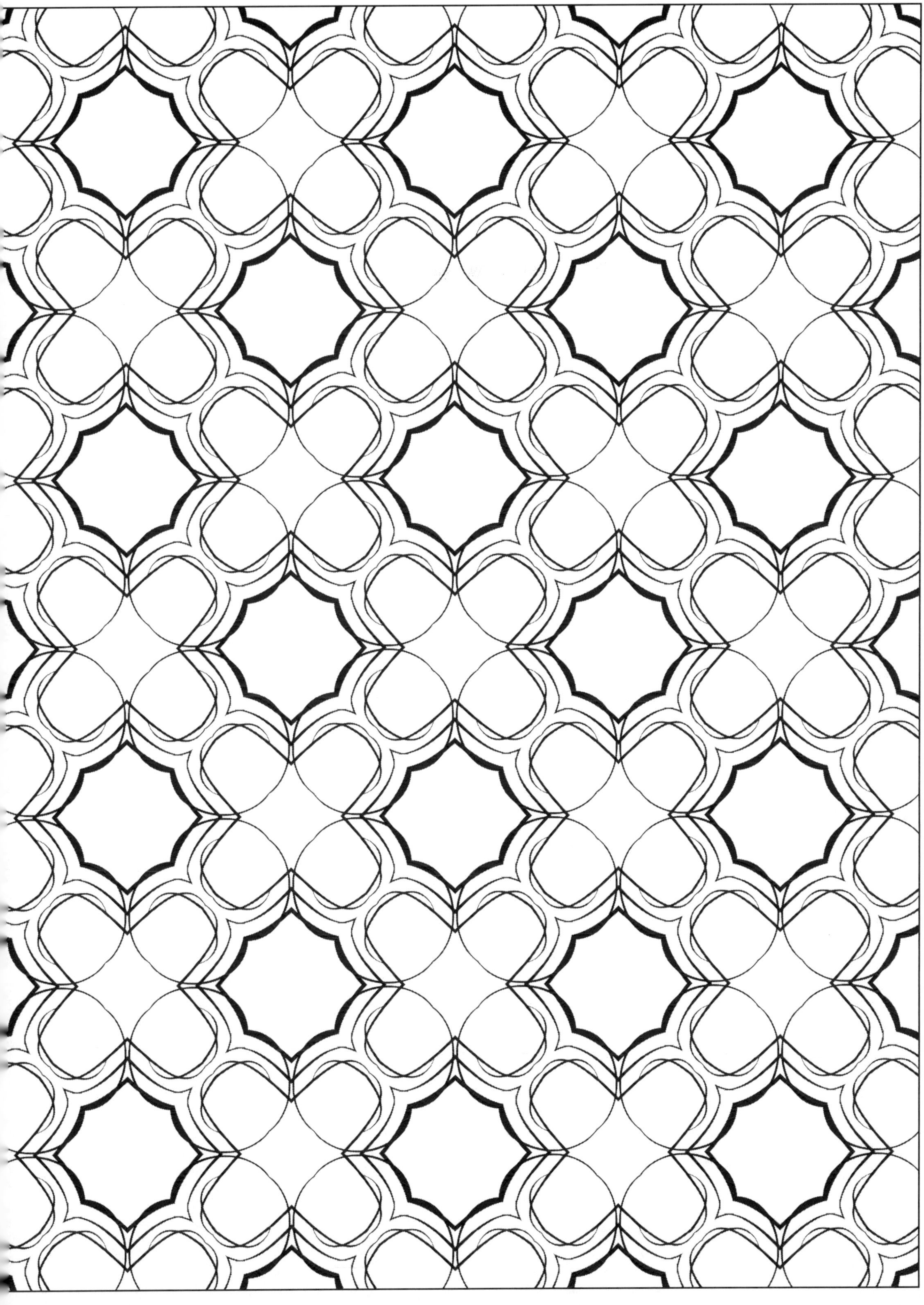

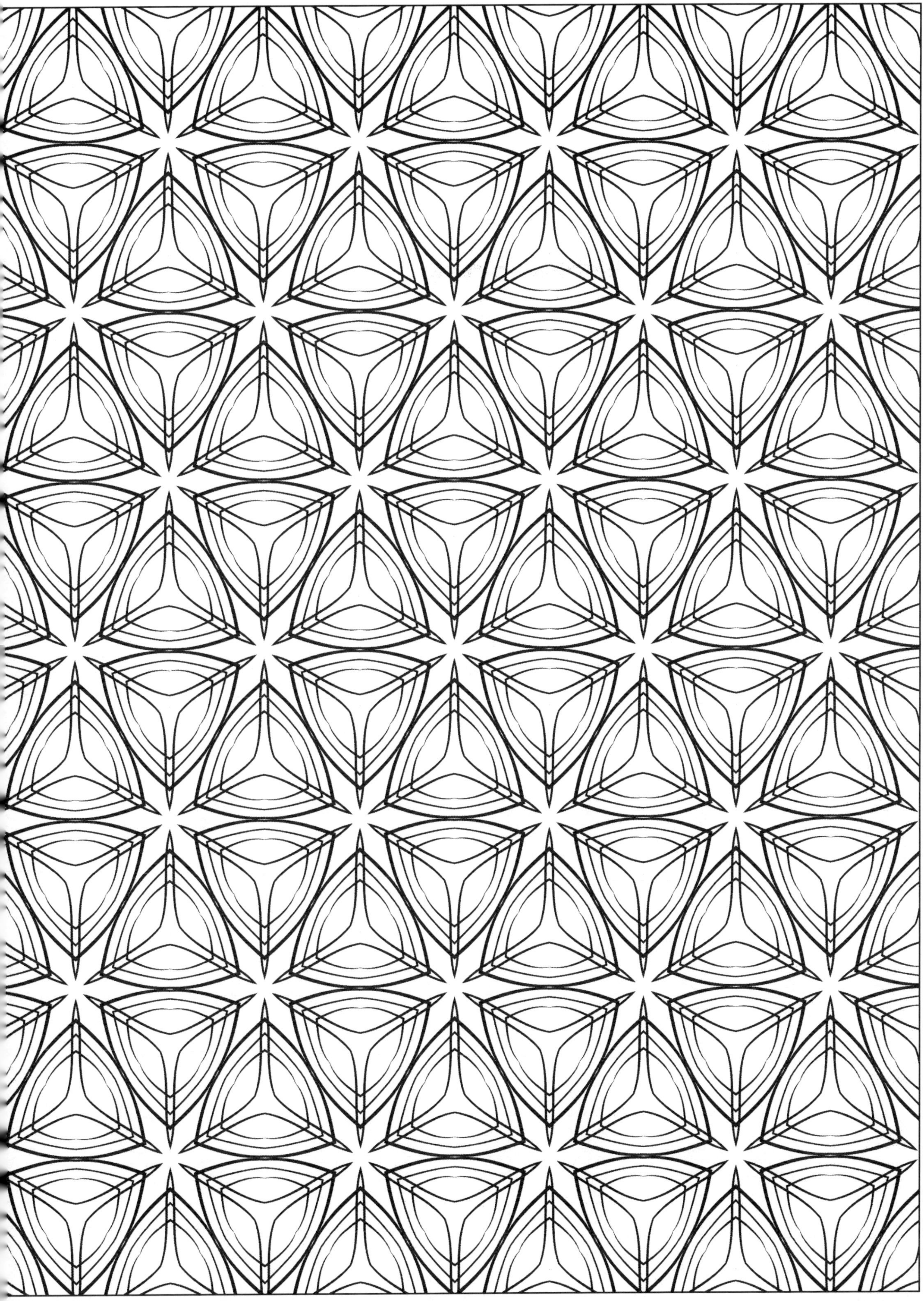

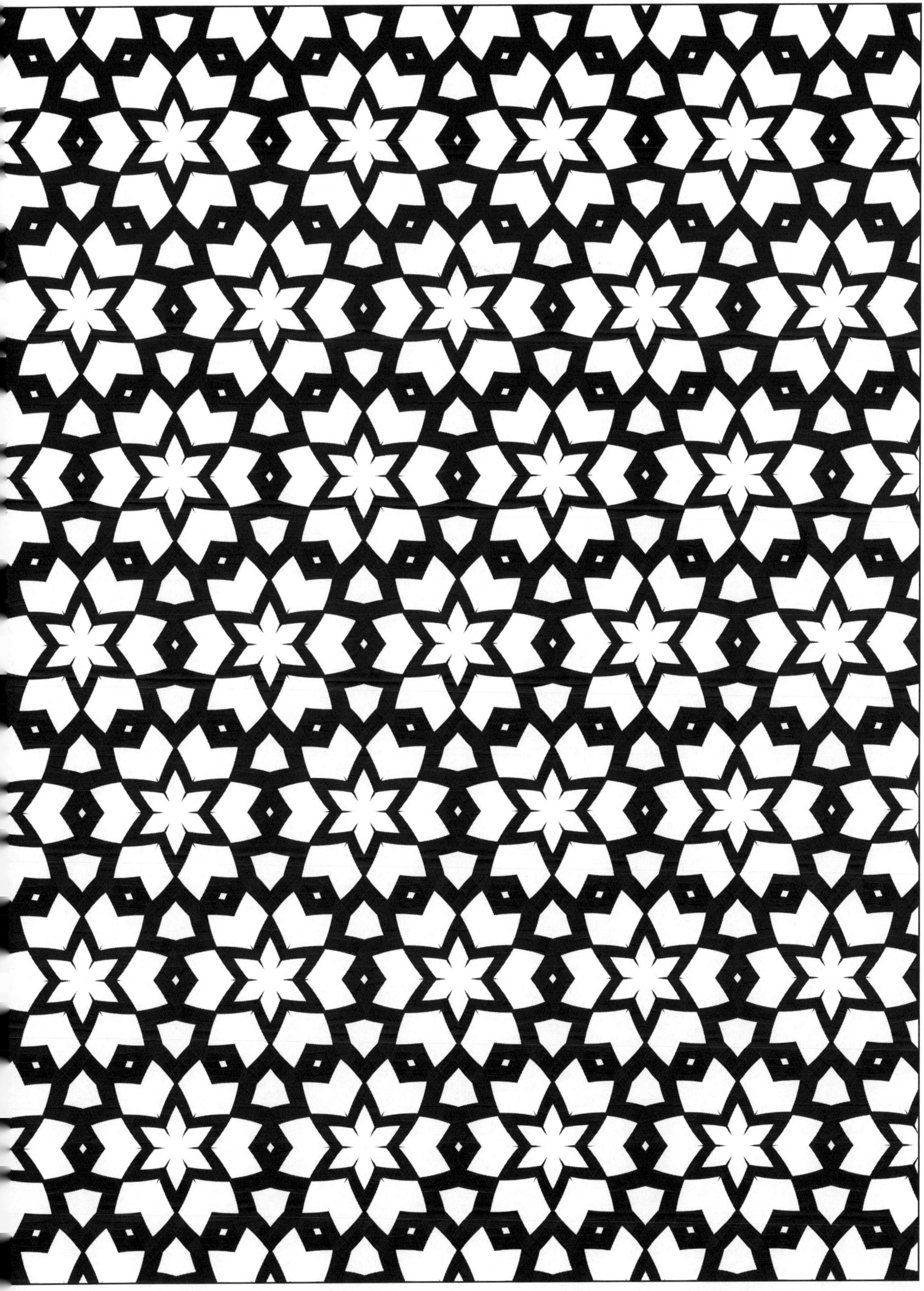

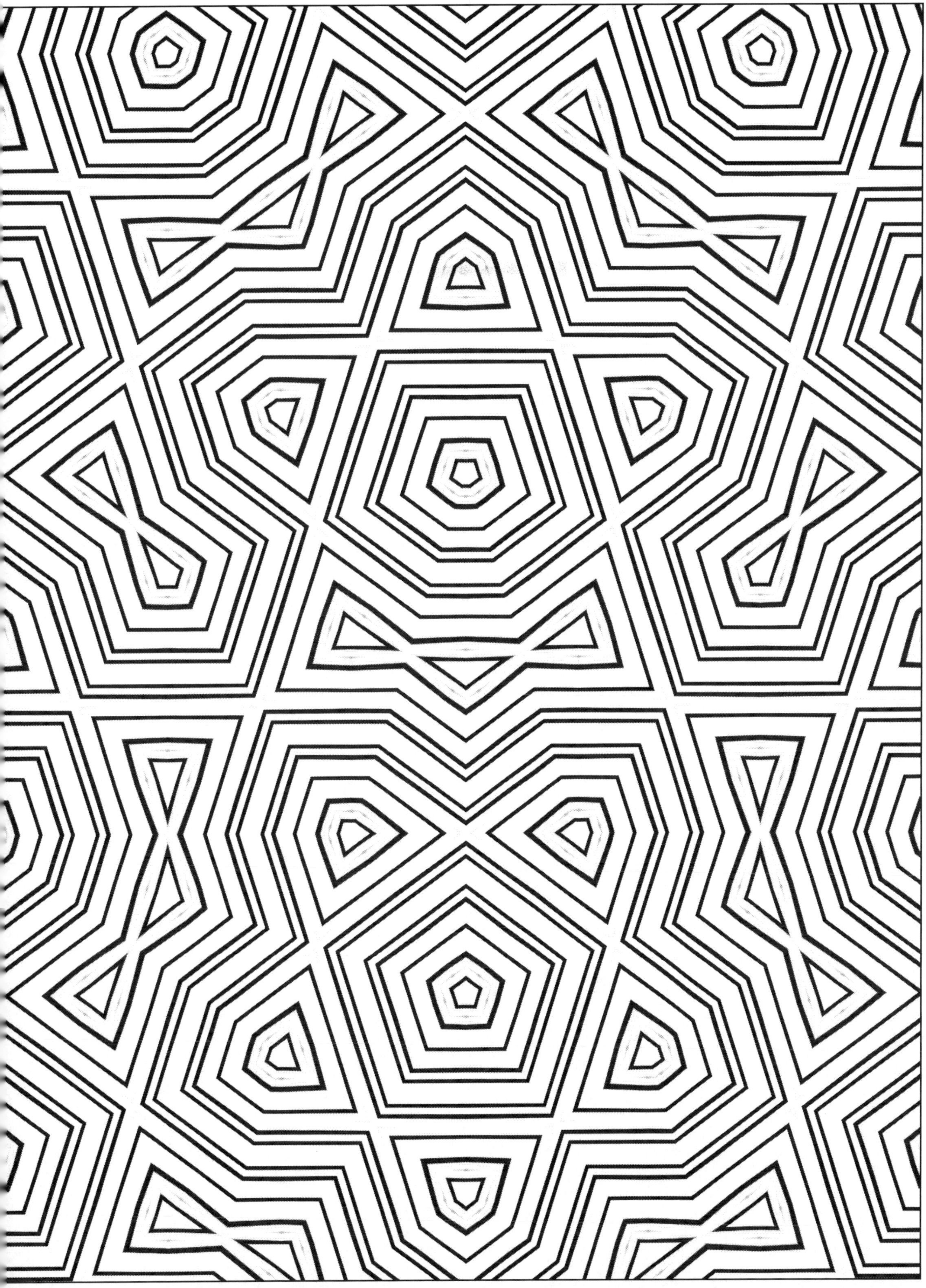

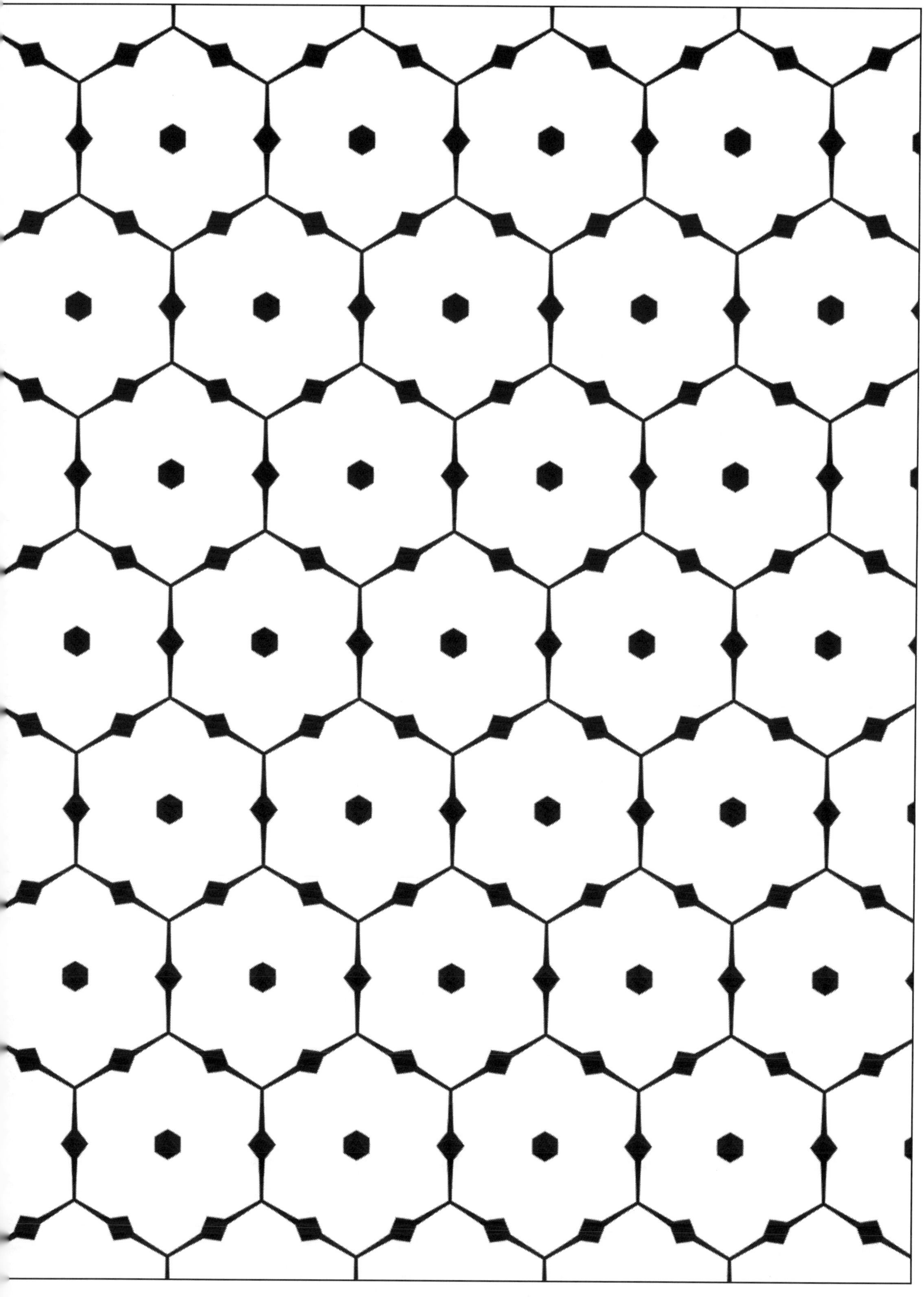

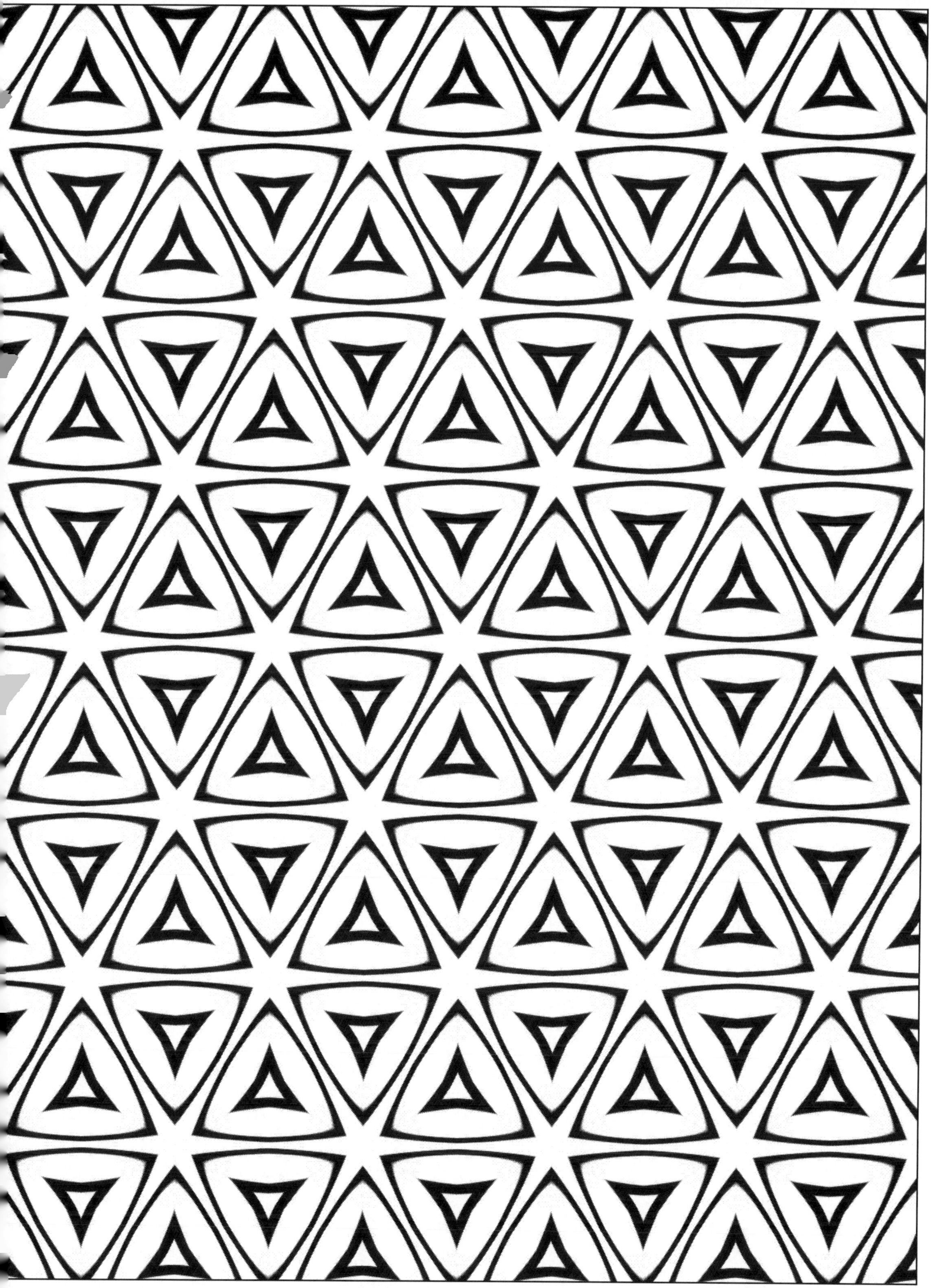

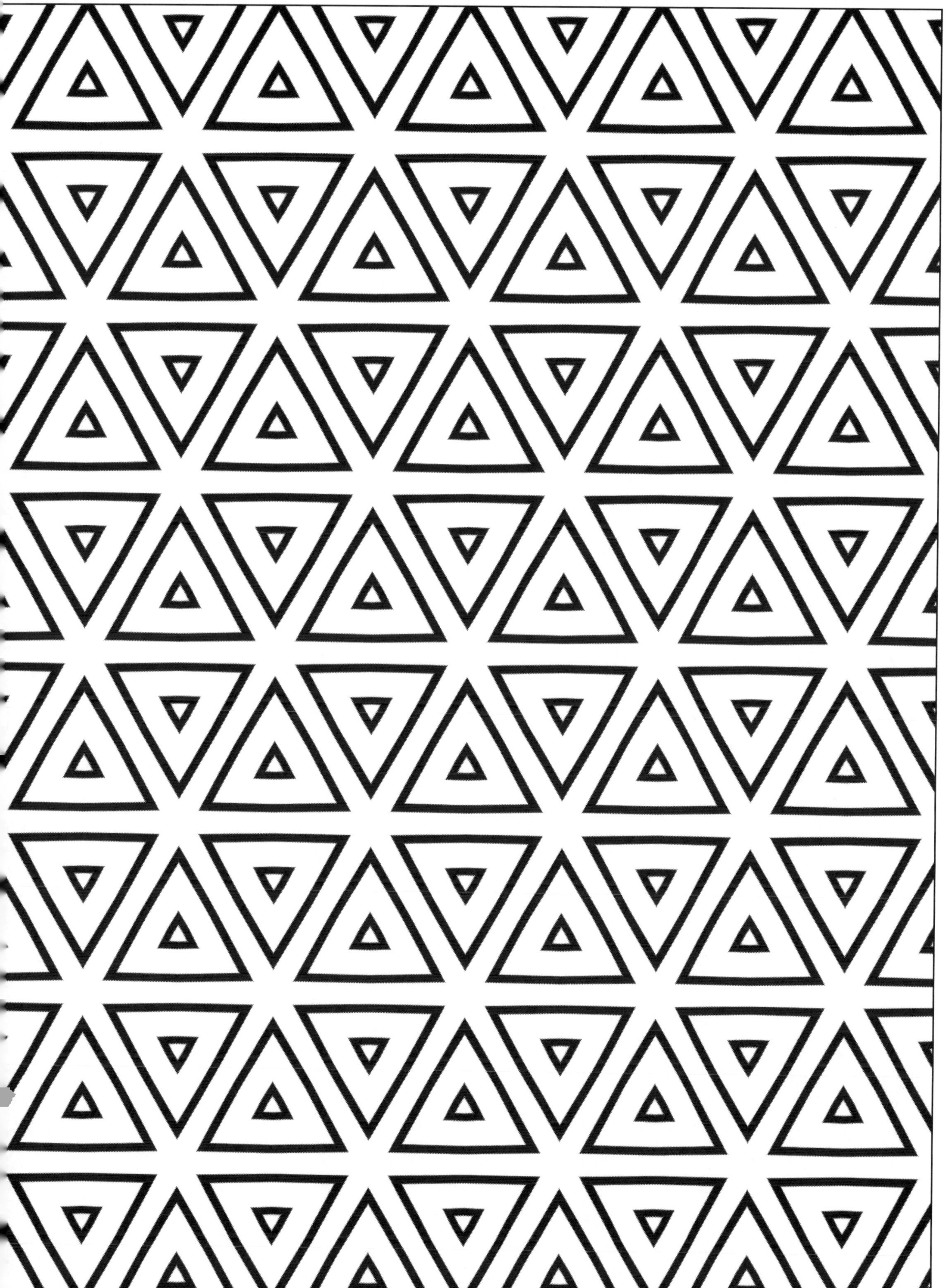

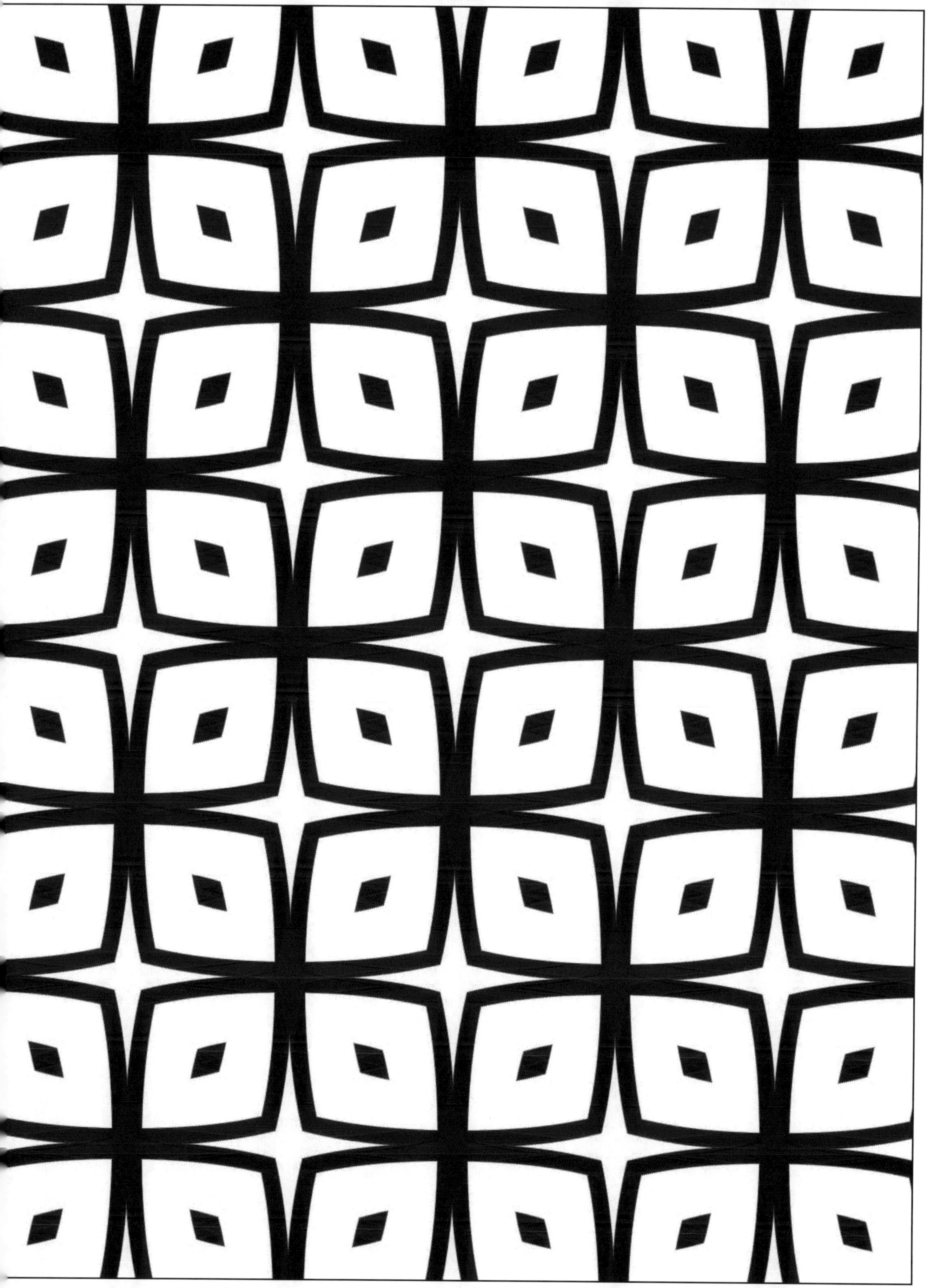

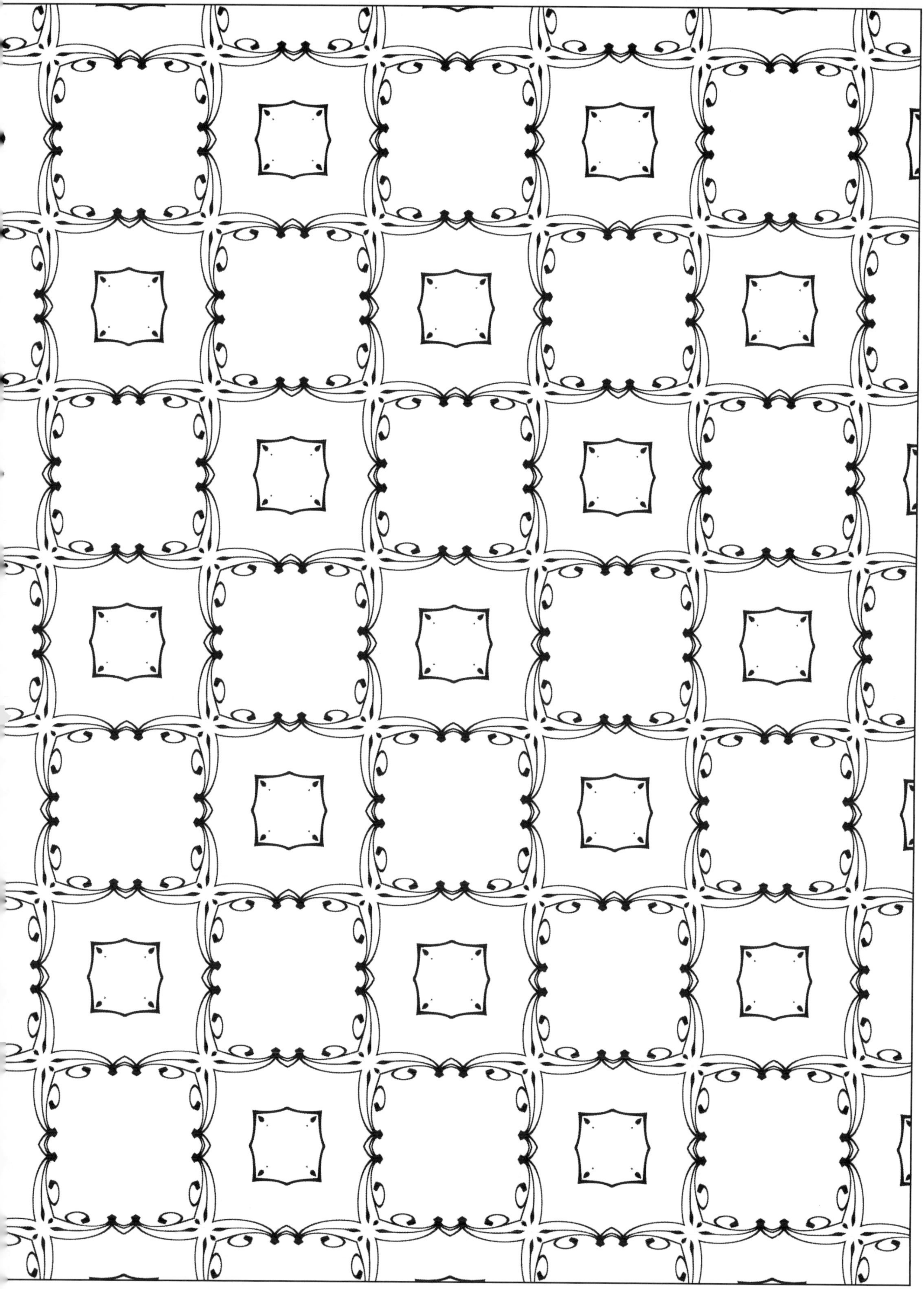

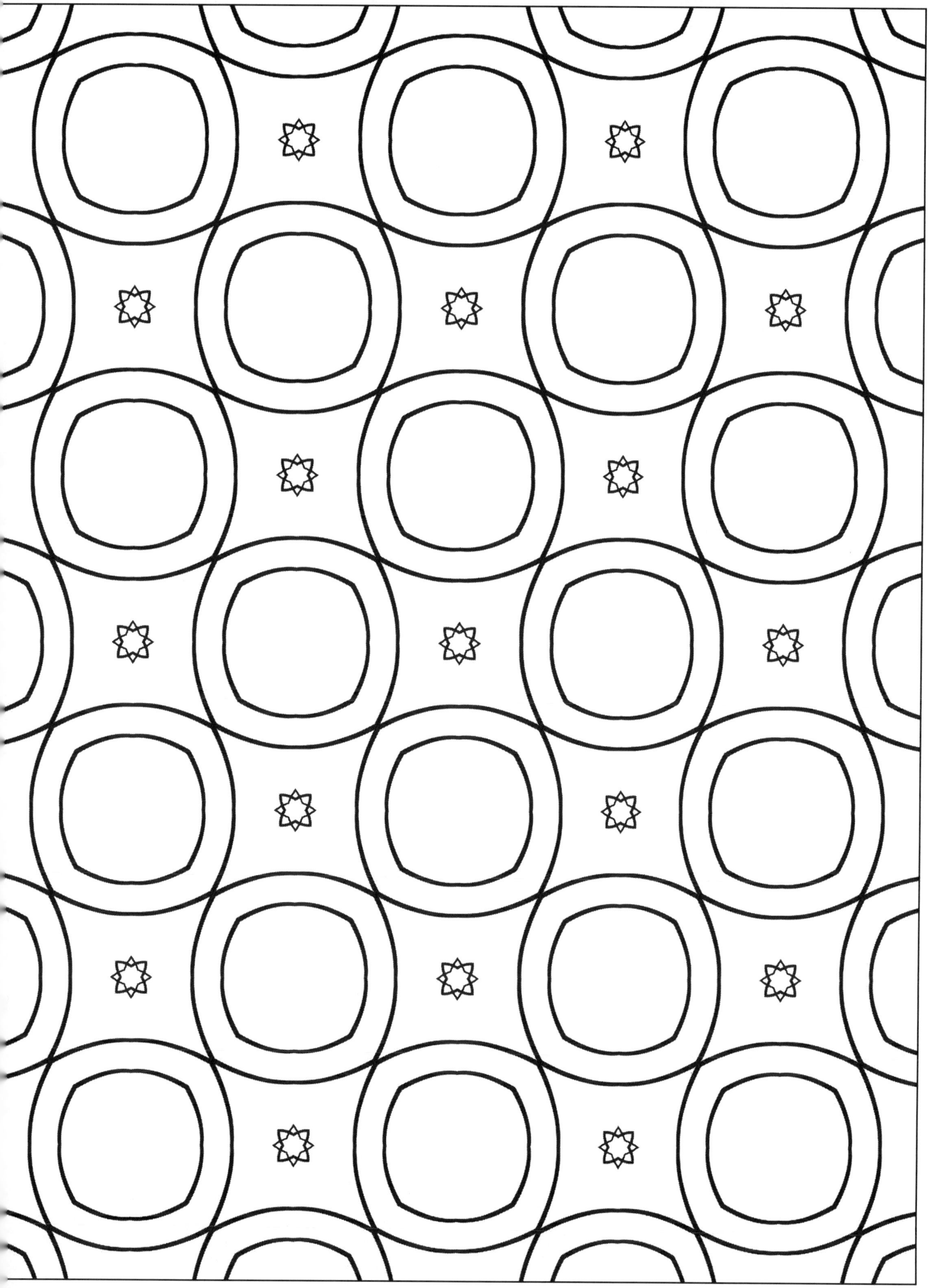

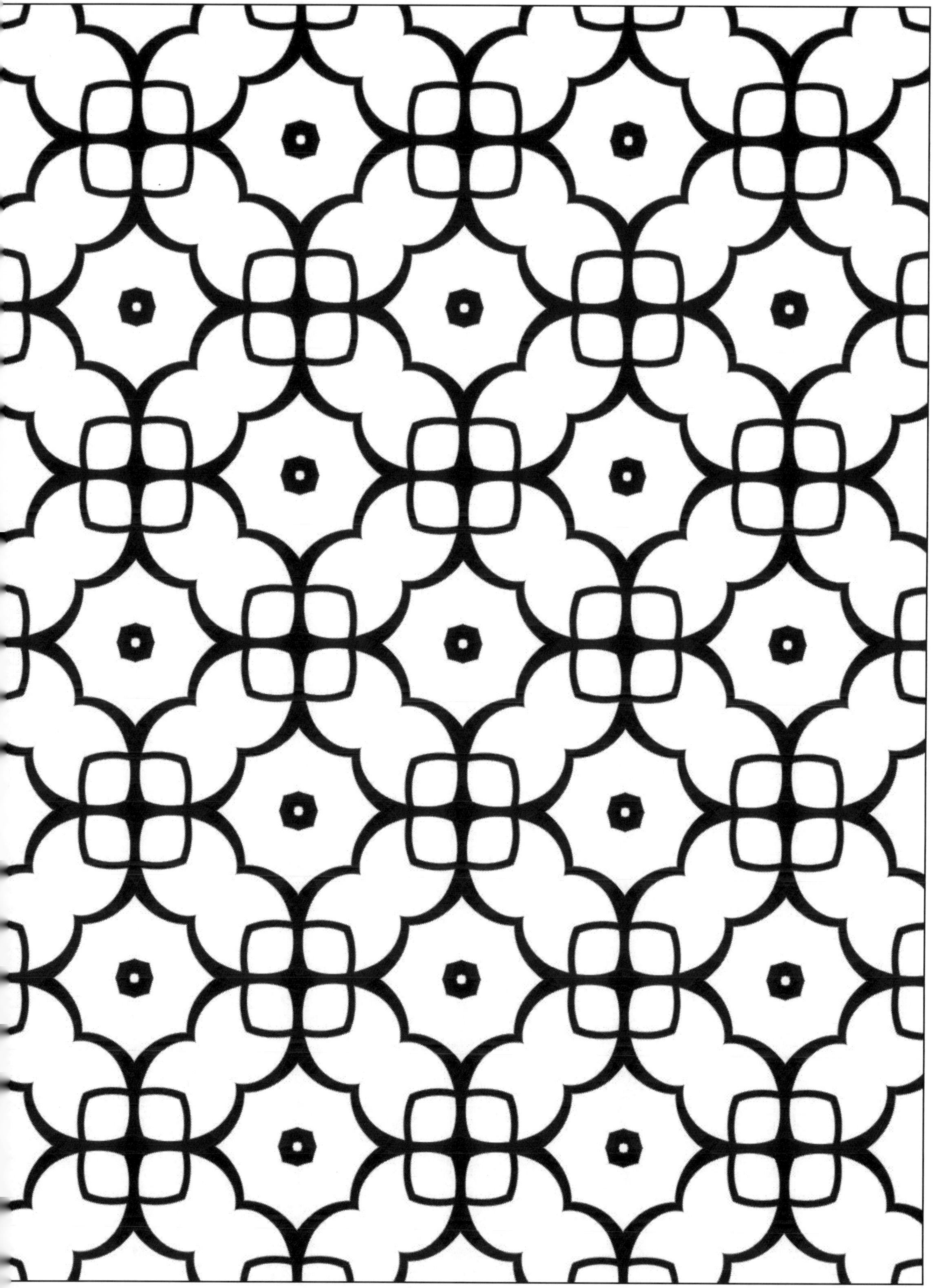

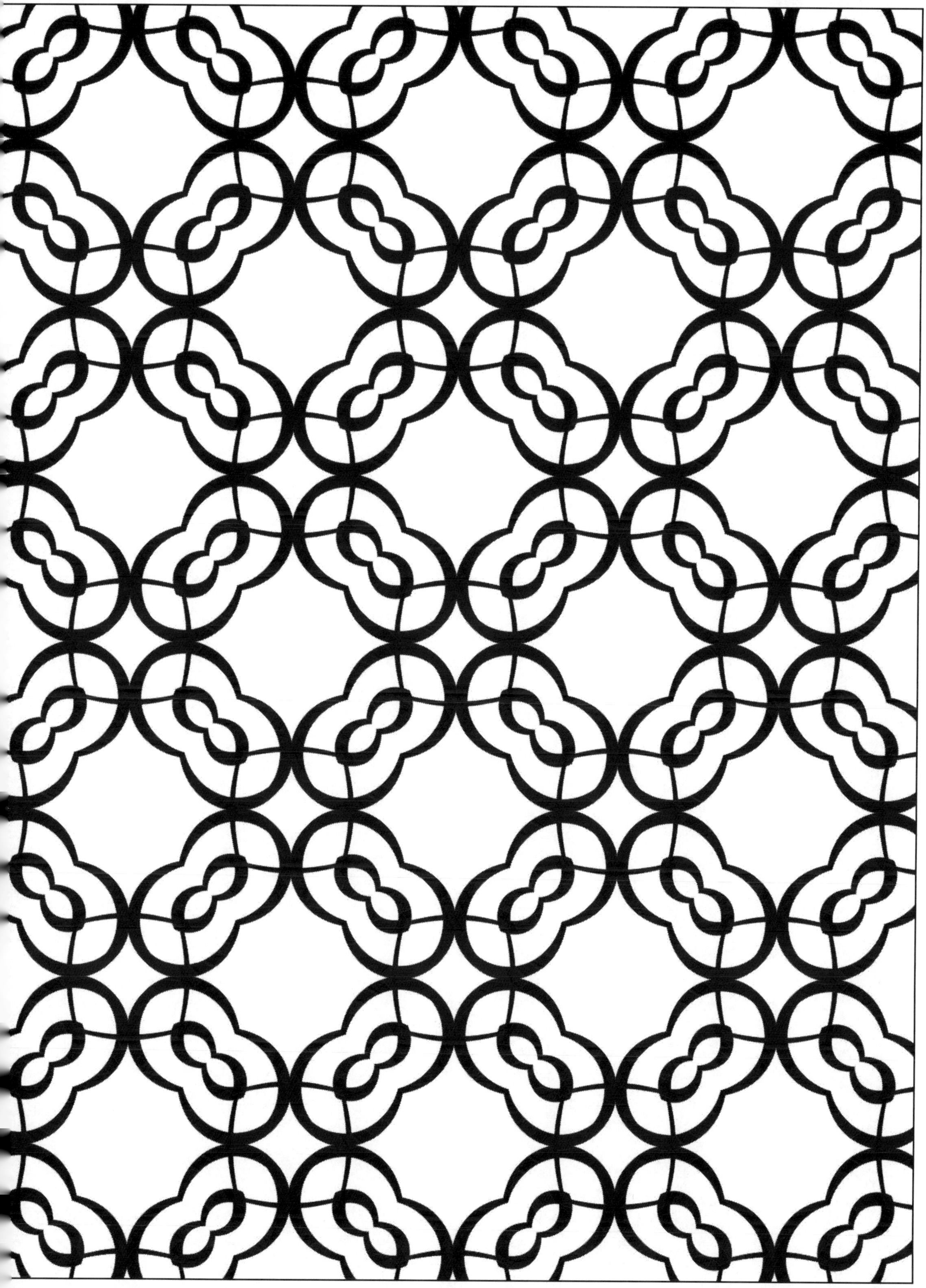

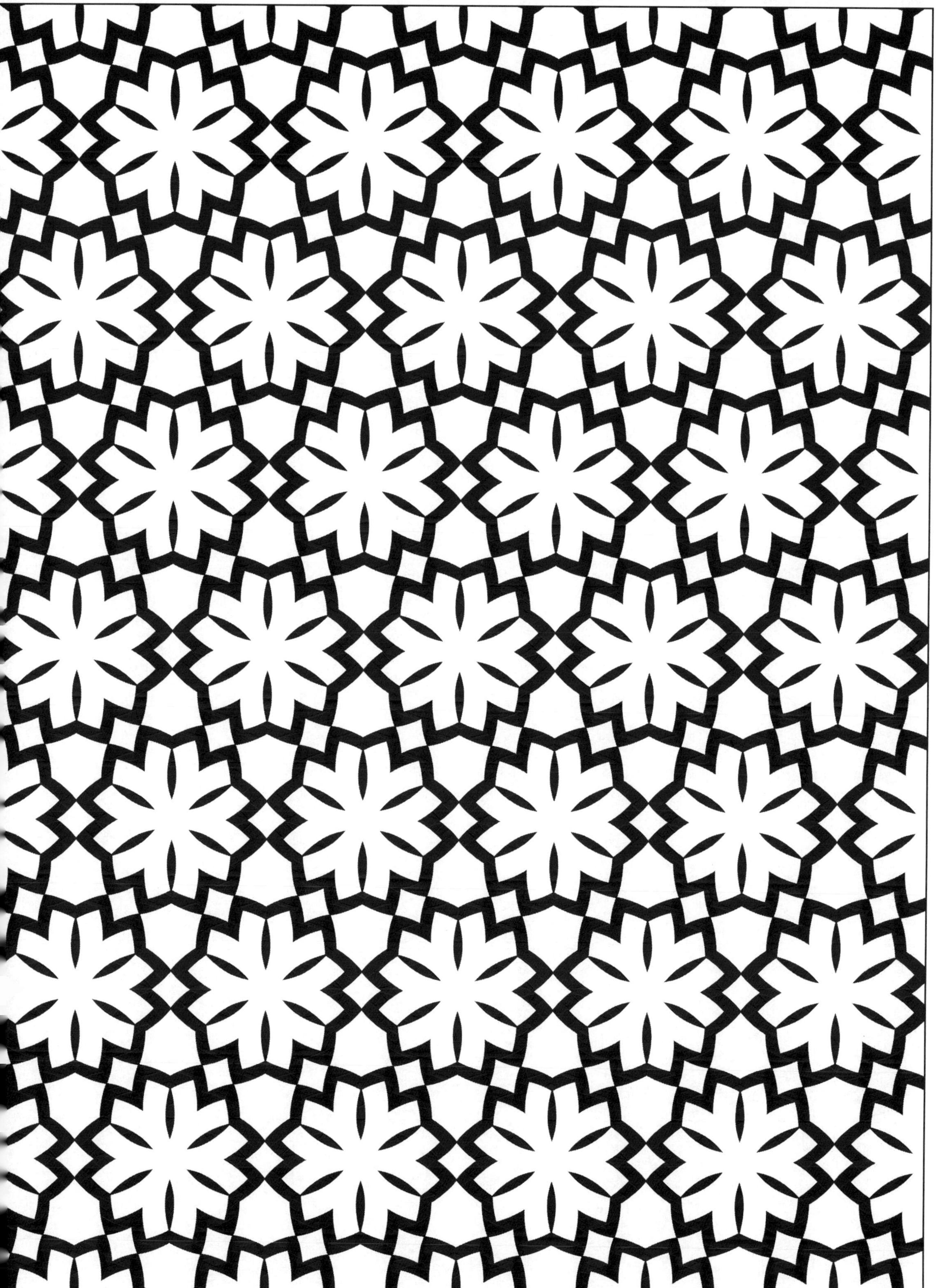

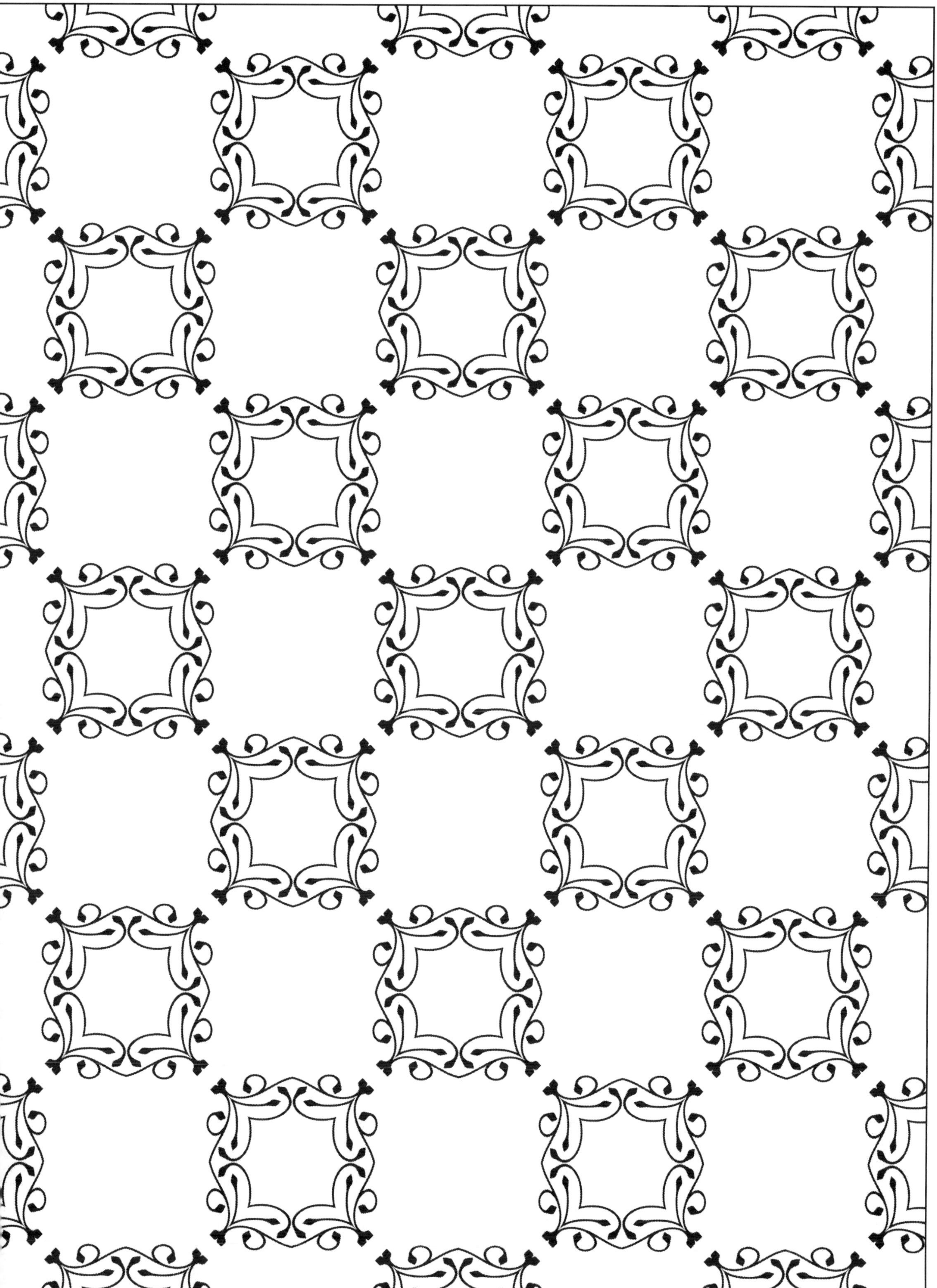

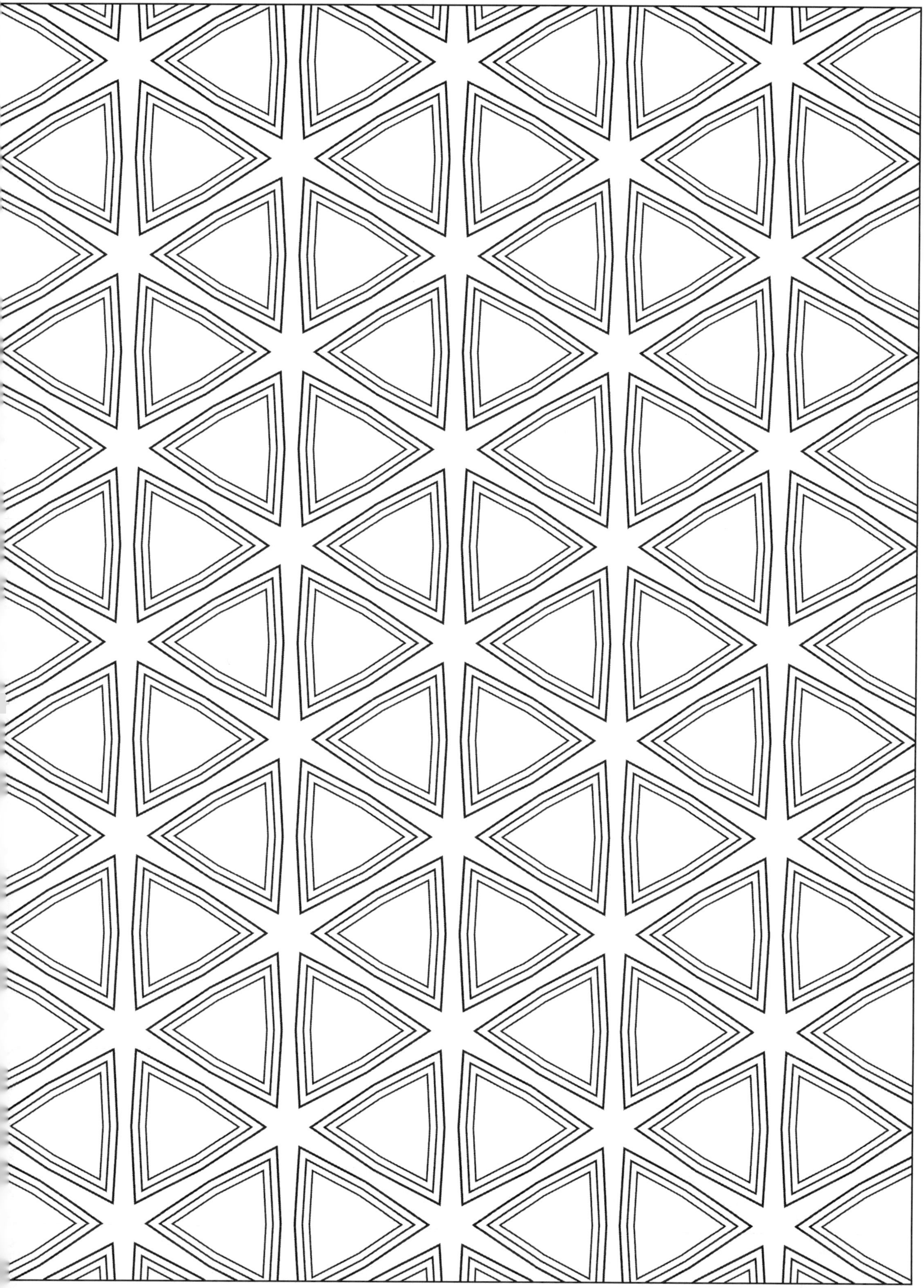

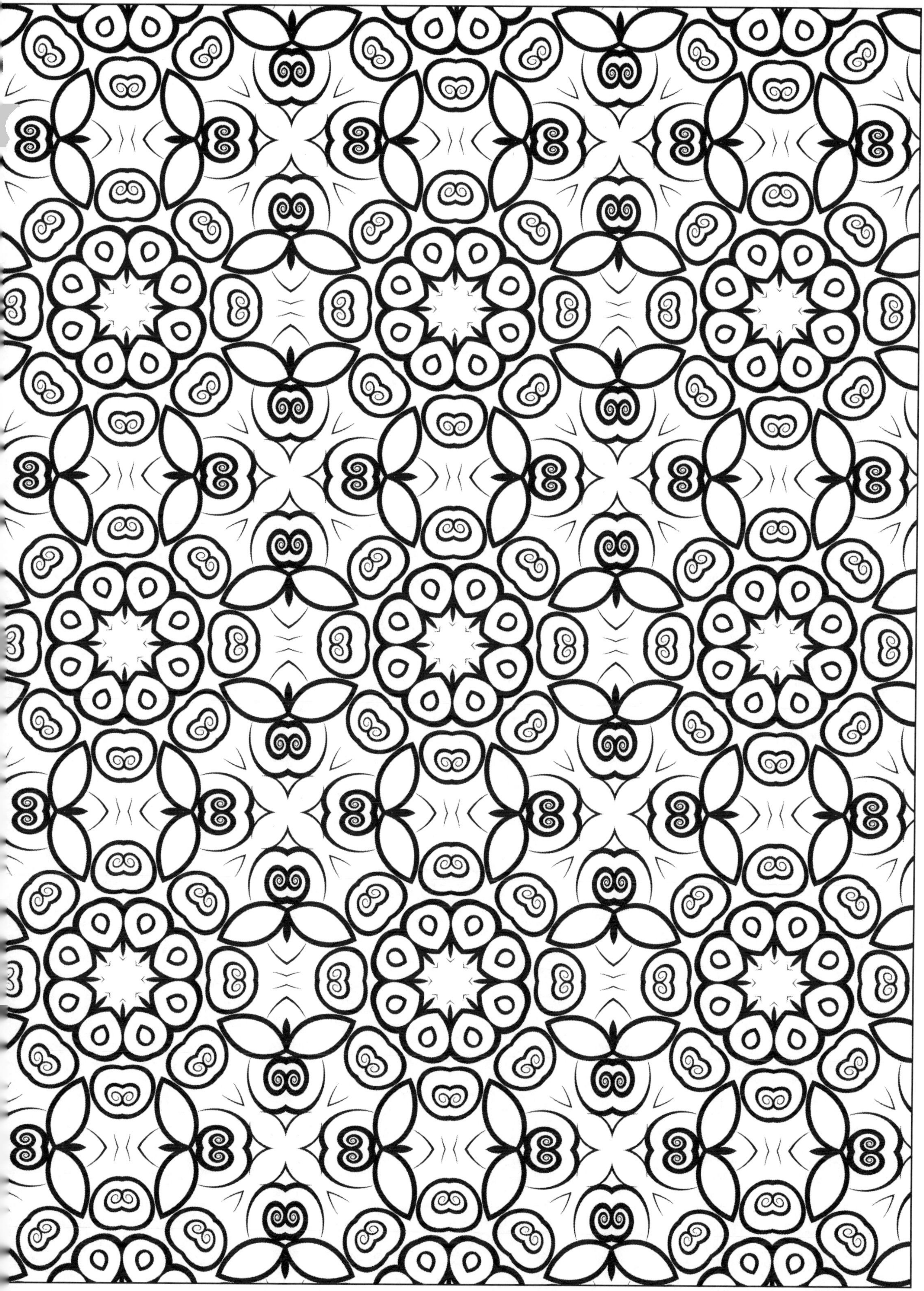

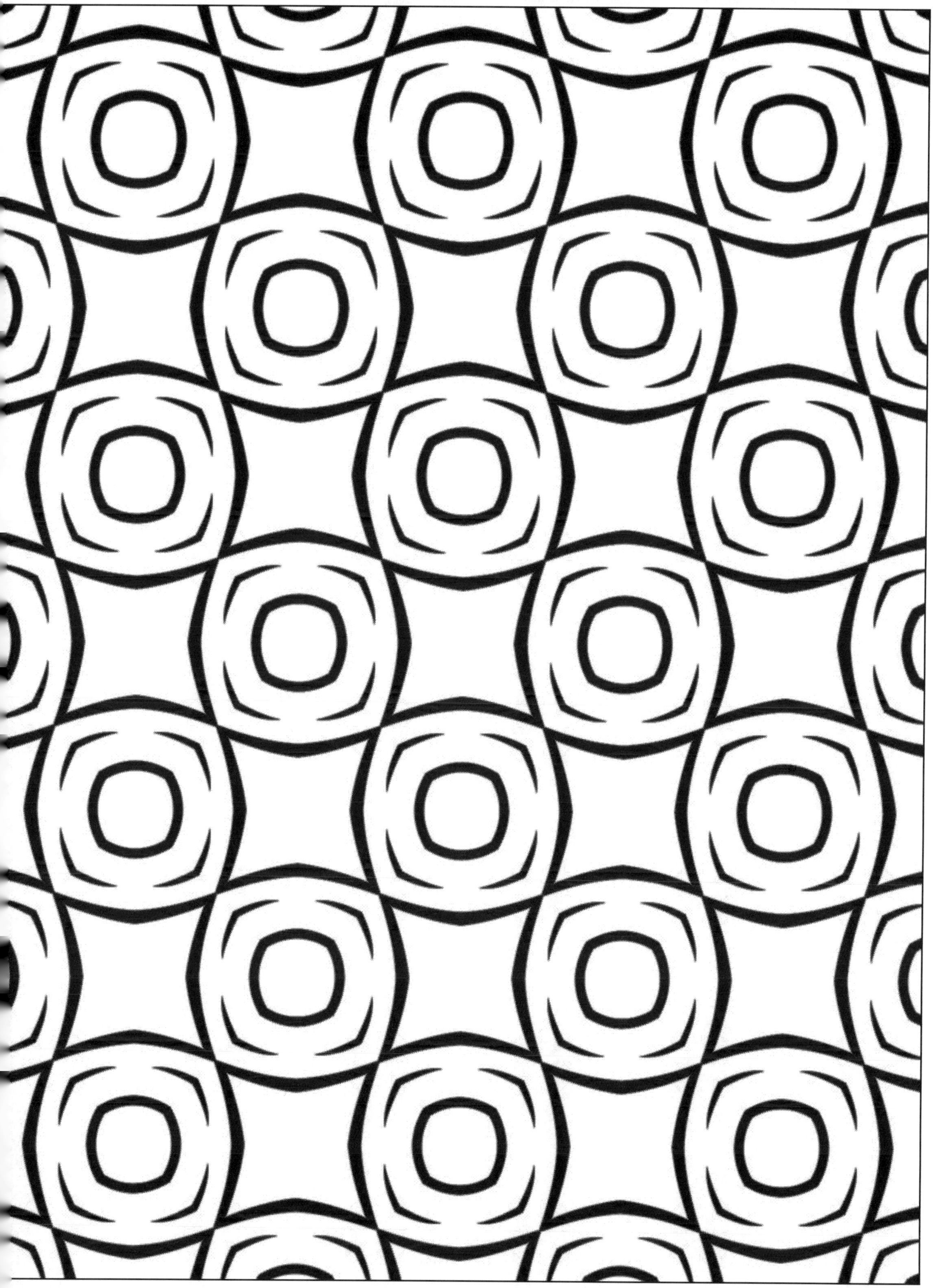

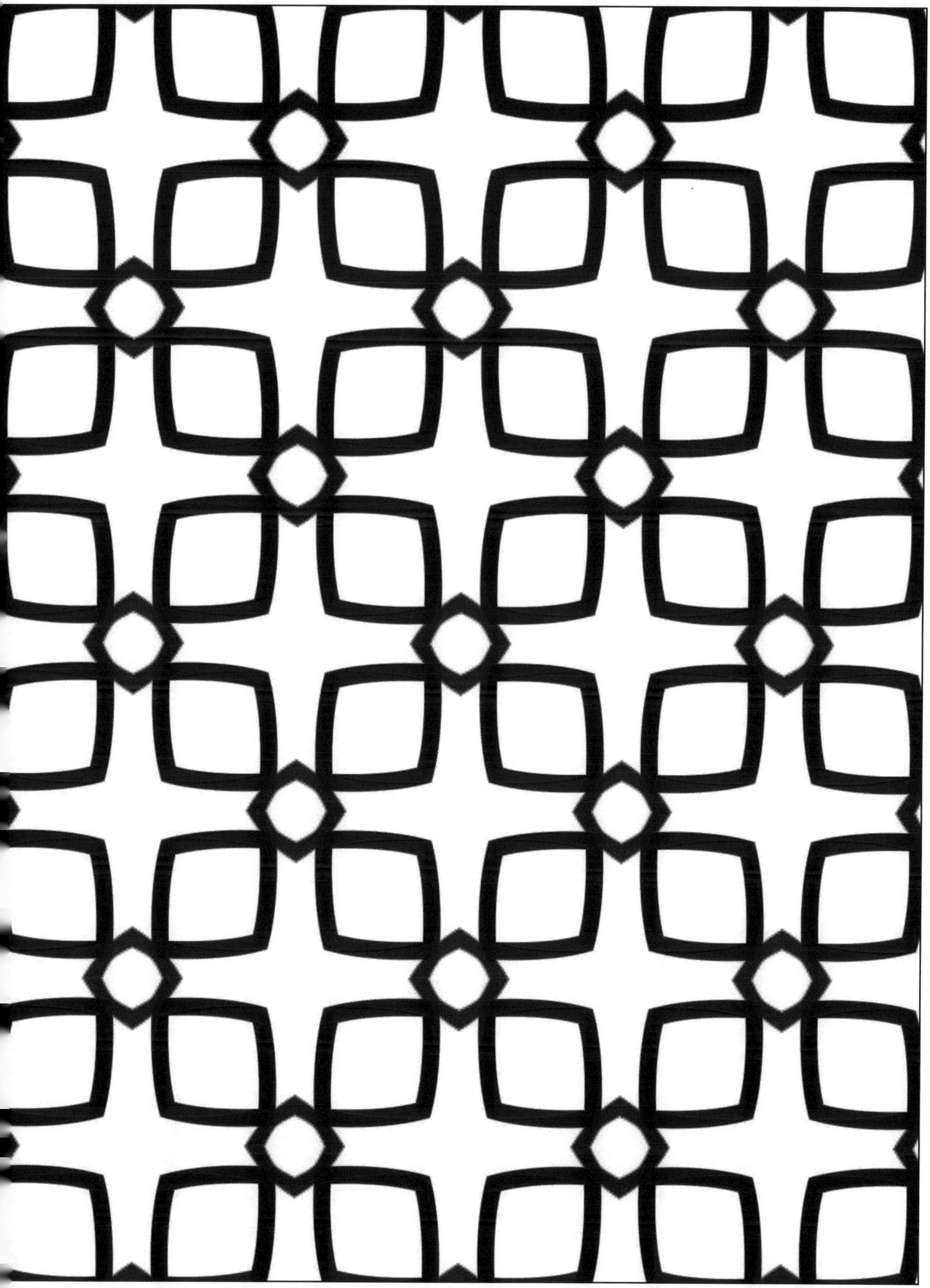

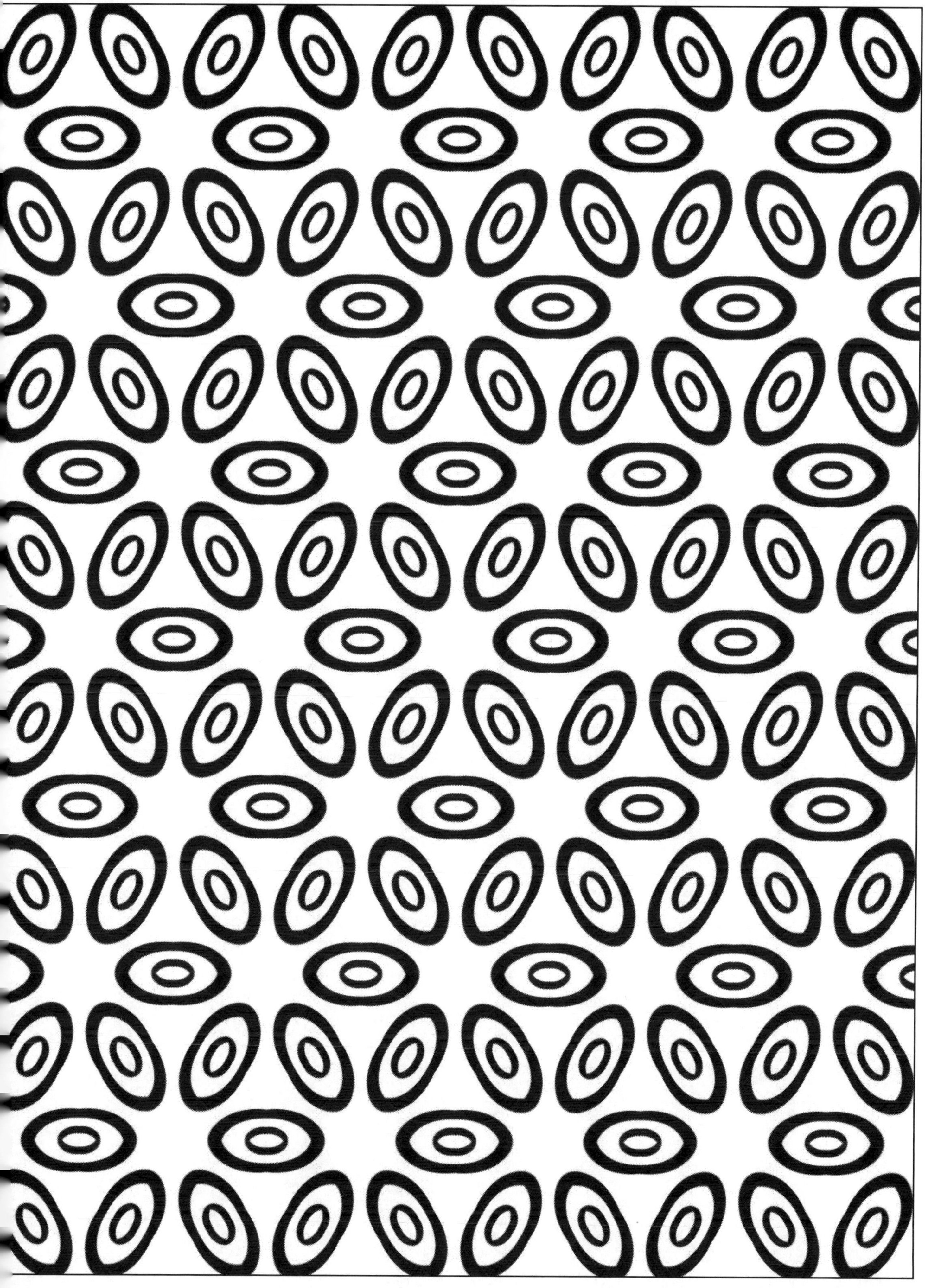

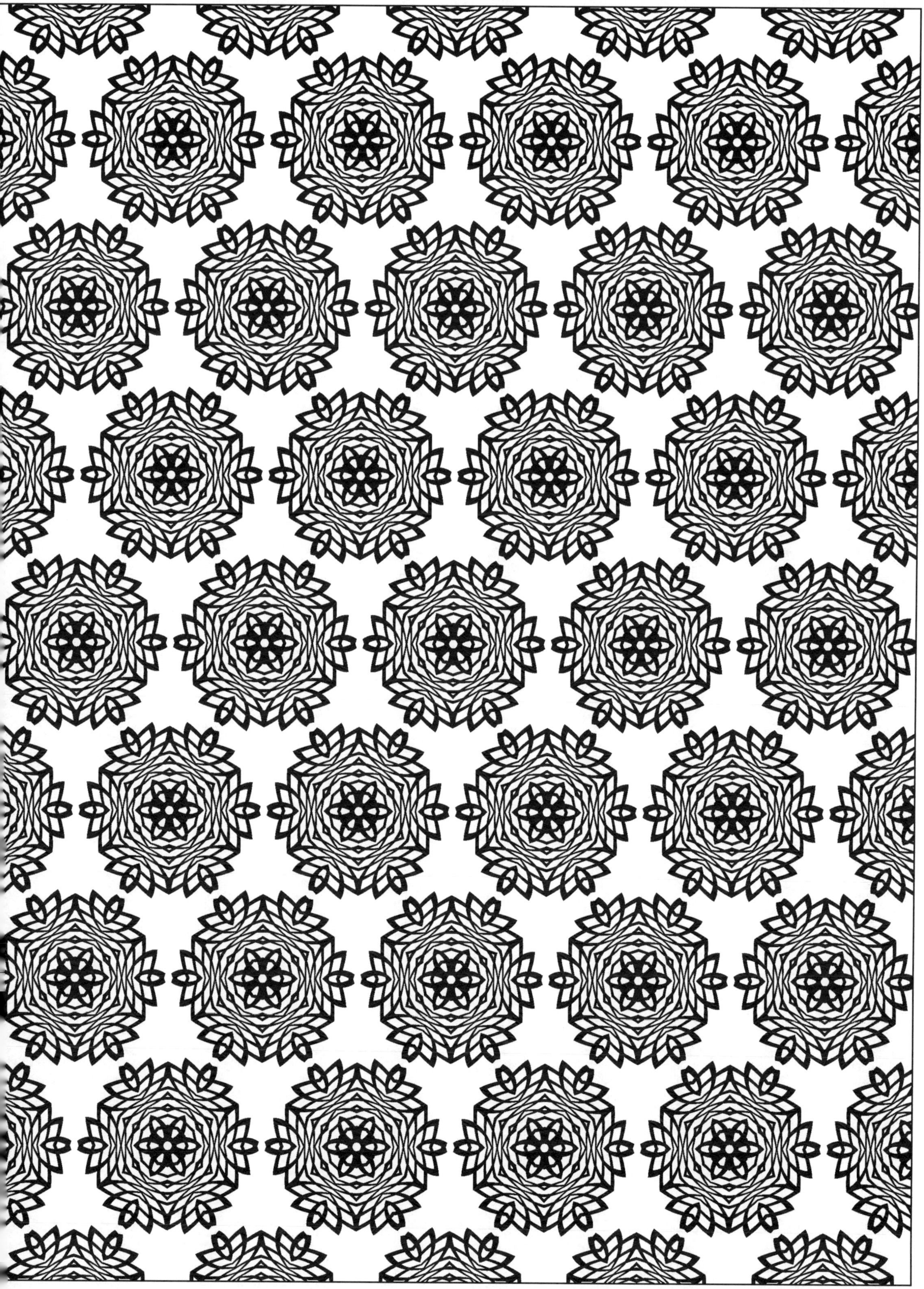

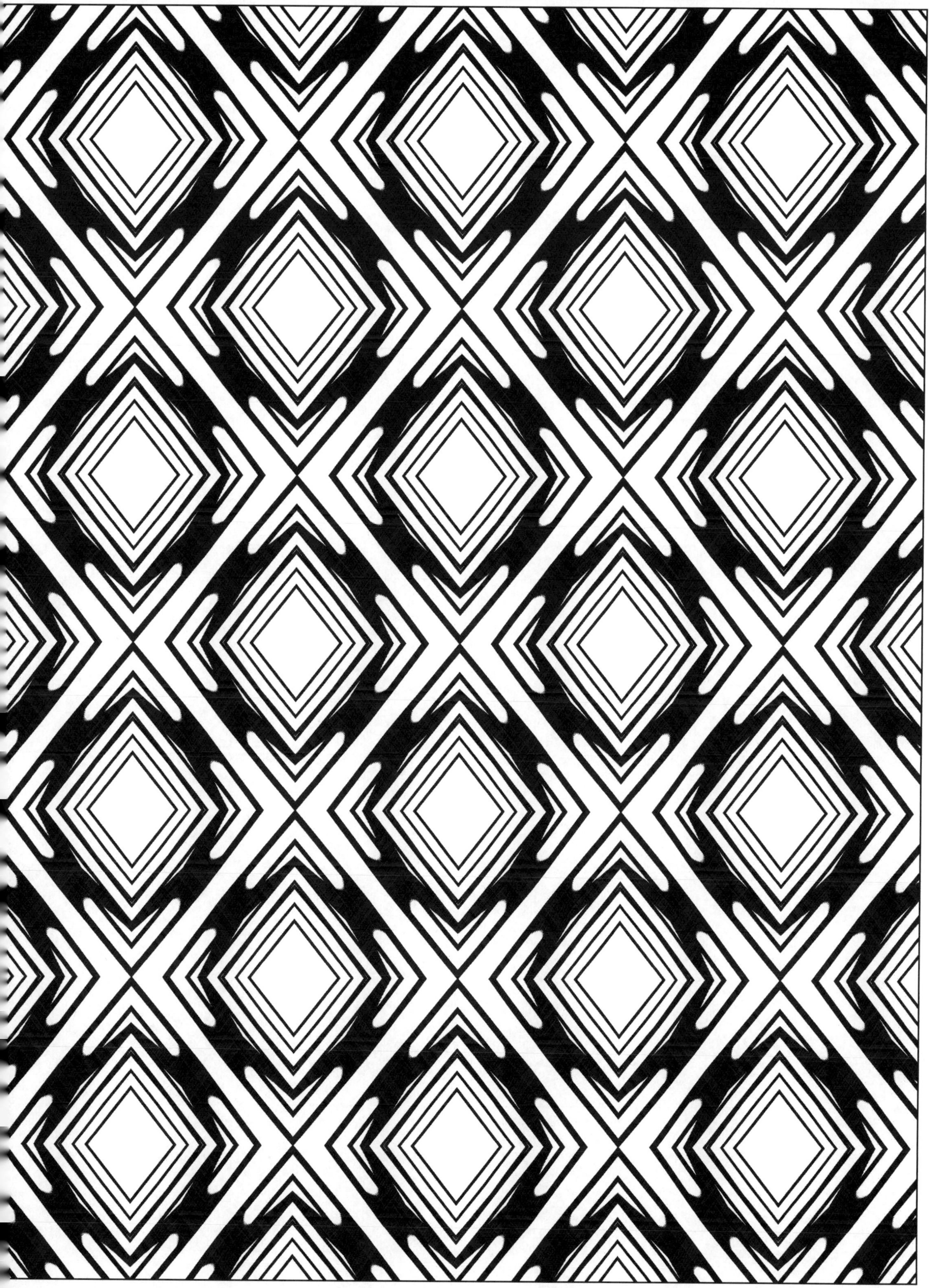

Made in United States
Orlando, FL
17 November 2024

54012238R00050